PRESIDENT'S MALARIA INITIATIVE

Mozambique

Malaria Operational Plan FY 2016

TABLE OF CONTENTS

ABBREVIATIONS and ACRONYMS

ACT	Artemisinin-based combination therapy
AIS	AIDS Indicator Survey
AL	Artemether-lumefantrine
ANC	Antenatal care
APE	*Agentes Polivalentes Elementares da Saúde*
BCC	Behavior change communication
BES	*Boletim Epidemiologico Semanal*
CDC	Centers for Disease Control and Prevention
CISM	*Centro de Investigação em Saude de Manhiça*
CMAM	Central Medical Stores
DEPROS	Health Promotion Department
DHS	Demographic and Health Survey
DPS	*Direcção Provincial de Saúde* (the Provincial Health Directorate)
EUV	End-use verification
FELTP	Field Epidemiology and Laboratory Training Program
FY	Fiscal year
GHI	Global Health Initiative
Global Fund	Global Fund to Fight AIDS, Tuberculosis and Malaria
GRM	Government of the Republic of Mozambique
HMIS	Health Management Information System
IEC	Information, education, communication
INE	*Instituto Nacional de Estatísticas*
INS	*Instituto Nacional de Saúde* (National Institute of Health)
IPTp	Intermittent preventive treatment for pregnant women
IRS	Indoor residual spraying
ITN	Insecticide-treated net
M&E	Monitoring and evaluation
MCH	Maternal and child health
MCSP	Maternal and Child Survival Project
MICS	Multiple Indicator Cluster Survey
MIP	Malaria in pregnancy
MIS	Malaria indicator survey
MoH	Ministry of Health
MOP	Malaria Operational Plan
MTR	Mid-term Review
NHS	National Health Service
NMCP	National Malaria Control Program
OR	Operational research
PCV	Peace Corps volunteer
PEPFAR	President's Emergency Plan for AIDS Relief
PIRCOM	Inter-Religious Campaign Against Malaria
PMI	President's Malaria Initiative
RDT	Rapid diagnostic test
SIMAM	*Sistema de Informação de Medicamentos e Artigos Médicos*

SIS-MA	*Sistema de Informação para a Saúde – Monitoria e Avaliação*
SP	Sulfadoxine-pyrimethamine
SPA	Service Provision Assessments
TES	Therapeutic efficacy study
UNICEF	United Nations Children's Fund
USAID	United States Agency for International Development
USG	United States Government
WHO	World Health Organization

I. EXECUTIVE SUMMARY

When it was launched in 2005, the goal of the President's Malaria Initiative (PMI) was to reduce malaria-related mortality by 50% across 15 high-burden countries in sub-Saharan Africa through a rapid scale-up of four proven and highly effective malaria prevention and treatment measures: insecticide-treated mosquito nets (ITNs); indoor residual spraying (IRS); accurate diagnosis and prompt treatment with artemisinin-based combination therapies (ACTs); and intermittent preventive treatment for pregnant women (IPTp). With the passage of the Tom Lantos and Henry J. Hyde Global Leadership against HIV/AIDS, Tuberculosis, and Malaria Act in 2008, PMI developed a U.S. Government Malaria Strategy for 2009–2014. This strategy included a long-term vision for malaria control in which sustained high coverage with malaria prevention and treatment interventions would progressively lead to malaria-free zones in Africa, with the ultimate goal of worldwide malaria eradication by 2040-2050. Consistent with this strategy and the increase in annual appropriations supporting PMI, four new sub-Saharan African countries and one regional program in the Greater Mekong Subregion of Southeast Asia were added in 2011. The contributions of PMI, together with those of other partners, have led to dramatic improvements in the coverage of malaria control interventions in PMI-supported countries, and all 15 original countries have documented substantial declines in all-cause mortality rates among children less than five years of age.

In 2015, PMI launched the next six-year strategy, setting forth a bold and ambitious goal and objectives. The PMI Strategy for 2015-2020 takes into account the progress over the past decade and the new challenges that have arisen. Malaria prevention and control remains a major U.S. foreign assistance objective and PMI's Strategy fully aligns with the U.S. Government's vision of ending preventable child and maternal deaths and ending extreme poverty. It is also in line with the goals articulated in the RBM Partnership's second generation global malaria action plan, *Action and Investment to defeat Malaria (AIM) 2016-2030: for a Malaria-Free World* and WHO's updated *Global Technical Strategy: 2016-2030*. Under the PMI Strategy 2015-2020, the U.S. Government's goal is to work with PMI-supported countries and partners to further reduce malaria deaths and substantially decrease malaria morbidity, towards the long-term goal of elimination.

Mozambique was selected as a PMI focus country in FY 2007.

This FY 2016 Malaria Operational Plan presents a detailed implementation plan for Mozambique, based on the strategies of PMI and the National Malaria Control Program (NMCP). It was developed in consultation with the NMCP and with the participation of national and international partners involved in malaria prevention and control in the country. The activities that PMI is proposing to support fit in well with the National Malaria Prevention and Control Strategic Plan and build on investments made by PMI and other partners to improve and expand malaria-related services, including the Global Fund to Fight AIDS, Tuberculosis, and Malaria (Global Fund). This document briefly reviews the current status of malaria control policies and interventions in Mozambique, describes progress to date, identifies challenges and unmet needs to achieving the targets of the NMCP and PMI, and provides a description of activities that are planned with FY 2016 funding.

The proposed FY 2016 PMI budget for Mozambique is $29 million. PMI will support the following intervention areas with these funds:

Insecticide-treated nets (ITNs):
The scale up of ITNs has been a cornerstone of Mozambique's vector control strategy, which calls for universal coverage throughout the country. Coverage and usage of nets by key target groups has increased since 2007, e.g., the number of children under five years of age using an ITN the previous night increased from 7% to 36%. However, the NMCP and its partners recognize that there is much more work needed to improve coverage and usage.

A national level universal coverage campaign will be carried out in 2017 with support from the Global Fund. To complement this effort, PMI's resources will be directed toward maintaining routine distribution of nets through ANC services in order to maintain coverage following the campaign.

Indoor residual spraying (IRS):
Indoor residual spraying is a core component of the NMCP's vector control strategy. While its geographic spread is limited, its coverage in terms of population is impressive with PMI covering nearly 10% of the country's population in 4 districts (440,579 structures). The recent emergence of data demonstrating resistance to pyrethroids has necessitated a change of insecticide to organophosphates, which are much more expensive than existing insecticide choices. In FY 2016, PMI will continue to support IRS activities in high burden areas with the Global Fund supporting insecticide procurement.

Malaria in pregnancy (MIP):
Prevention of malaria in pregnant women, through the use of sulfadoxine-pyrimethamine (SP) for IPTp and ITN distribution, has been promoted in Mozambique since 2006 and implemented through the "Integrated Reproductive Health/Maternal-Neonatal-Child Services Package" since 2012. PMI has supported the development of national policies and guidelines through training, improvement of the quality of care, and revision of maternal and child health (MCH) registers.

With FY 2016 funding, PMI will: 1) Continue to provide central level support for MIP policy and planning, with an increased focus on the provincial and district level and an expanded geographic area; 2) Provide support and on-the-ground mentoring to *Direcção Provincial de Saúde* (DPS) staff to ensure rigorous supervision and training is provided to ANC staff to provide a comprehensive package of malaria interventions to pregnant women; and 3) Focus on the collection and reporting of key MIP indicators.

Case management:
The national malaria treatment guidelines require parasitological diagnosis of fever before treatment with an antimalarial, in line with WHO policy. However, access to quality diagnosis and treatment is still extremely low throughout the country. Supply gaps, training and supervision needs, as well as access to facilities, all play a role in this —particularly in the highly endemic north of the country. PMI and the Global Fund are the primary suppliers of ACTs and rapid diagnostic tests (RDTs) in Mozambique. Additionally, with PMI's support to the delivery system of health facility kits, stock levels are steadily improving.

In FY 2016, PMI will continue to support the procurement of RDTs and ACTs, which are pooled with Global Fund commodities and distributed through government systems. These systems will be supported further with provincial and district health managers capacitated to improve their use of data and planning to bridge quality gaps. PMI will also continue to support the strengthening of laboratory services.

Health systems strengthening and capacity building:
The health system in Mozambique is still recovering from the Civil War, and critical gaps still remain in staff capacity, planning and monitoring. PMI has been steadily consolidating its approach to health systems support in Mozambique and will take that further in FY 2016 with direct support to four of the most highly endemic provinces (Tete, Zambezia, Nampula and Cabo Delgado). FY 2016 funds will support provincial and district managers to better collect, interpret and act on health system data, which will also be strengthened. Supervision and capacity building at the facility level will be improved to increase quality of care while also addressing systemic gaps in service provision.

Behavior change communication (BCC):
The Mozambican Ministry of Health (MoH) recognizes BCC as an area in urgent need of direction and investment. Low rates of ITN use and poor treatment seeking behavior suggest a change of direction is needed. In this light the NMCP's communication working group has made recent strides to harmonize messaging and delivery channels in line with the recent World Malaria Day. PMI's FY 2016 funding will support the continuation of the development of these central level coordination efforts in addition to an increased focus on high quality community level approaches to better promote the uptake of desired behaviors.

Monitoring and evaluation (M&E):
Mozambique has strong monitoring and evaluation (M&E) activities. PMI support aligns with the NMCP 2012-2016 M&E Plan. Sources of data and information include the routine health information system, integrated disease surveillance, activity reports from districts, and periodic household and facility surveys.

A combined AIDS Indicator Survey/ Malaria Indicator Survey is ongoing in 2015. A health facility survey is also planned for later in 2015. PMI plans to continue support for end-use verification surveys, ITN monitoring, entomologic monitoring, therapeutic efficacy studies, and training two Field Epidemiology and Laboratory Training Program residents per year. In addition, the Mozambique Impact Evaluation report is anticipated in August 2015.

With FY 2016 funding, PMI will focus more on routine health information by supporting the transition to DHIS-2 in four provinces. PMI will work to strengthen data collection, reporting, analysis, and data use at the health facility, district, provincial, and central levels to enable data-driven decision-making.

Operational research (OR):
PMI will use FY2016 funds to investigate the effectiveness of IRS alone when compared to its use when combined with ITNs in areas of confirmed pyrethroid resistance. As per the national

strategy, none of these districts will receive ITNs until 2017, providing a unique opportunity to investigate the additional benefit of both interventions together in areas of pyrethroid resistance. This activity will monitor the effect of changing from IRS only to IRS with the addition of nets in terms of both entomological and epidemiological indicators.

II. STRATEGY

1. Introduction

When it was launched in 2005, the goal of PMI was to reduce malaria-related mortality by 50% across 15 high-burden countries in sub-Saharan Africa through a rapid scale-up of four proven and highly effective malaria prevention and treatment measures: insecticide-treated mosquito nets (ITNs); indoor residual spraying (IRS); accurate diagnosis and prompt treatment with artemisinin-based combination therapies (ACTs); and intermittent preventive treatment for pregnant women (IPTp). With the passage of the Tom Lantos and Henry J. Hyde Global Leadership against HIV/AIDS, Tuberculosis, and Malaria Act in 2008, PMI developed a U.S. Government Malaria Strategy for 2009–2014. This strategy included a long-term vision for malaria control in which sustained high coverage with malaria prevention and treatment interventions would progressively lead to malaria-free zones in Africa, with the ultimate goal of worldwide malaria eradication by 2040-2050. Consistent with this strategy and the increase in annual appropriations supporting PMI, four new sub-Saharan African countries and one regional program in the Greater Mekong Subregion of Southeast Asia were added in 2011. The contributions of PMI, together with those of other partners, have led to dramatic improvements in the coverage of malaria control interventions in PMI-supported countries, and all 15 original countries have documented substantial declines in all-cause mortality rates among children less than five years of age.

In 2015, PMI launched the next six-year strategy, setting forth a bold and ambitious goal and objectives. The PMI Strategy for 2015-2020 takes into account the progress over the past decade and the new challenges that have arisen. Malaria prevention and control remains a major U.S. foreign assistance objective and PMI's Strategy fully aligns with the U.S. Government's vision of ending preventable child and maternal deaths and ending extreme poverty. It is also in line with the goals articulated in the RBM Partnership's second generation global malaria action plan, *Action and Investment to defeat Malaria (AIM) 2016-2030: for a Malaria-Free World* and WHO's updated *Global Technical Strategy: 2016-2030.* Under the PMI Strategy 2015-2020, the U.S. Government's goal is to work with PMI-supported countries and partners to further reduce malaria deaths and substantially decrease malaria morbidity, towards the long-term goal of elimination.

Mozambique was selected as a PMI focus country in FY 2007.

This FY 2016 Malaria Operational Plan presents a detailed implementation plan for Mozambique, based on the strategies of PMI and the National Malaria Control Program (NMCP) strategy. It was developed in consultation with the NMCP and with the participation of national and international partners involved in malaria prevention and control in the country. The activities that PMI is proposing to support fit in well with the National Malaria Prevention and Control Strategic Plan and build on investments made by PMI and other partners to improve and expand malaria-related services, including the Global Fund to Fight AIDS, Tuberculosis, and Malaria (Global Fund). This document briefly reviews the current status of malaria control policies and interventions in Mozambique, describes progress to date, identifies challenges and unmet needs to achieving the targets of the NMCP and PMI, and provides a description of activities that are planned with FY 2016 funding.

2. Malaria situation in Mozambique

Malaria is endemic throughout Mozambique, and its entire estimated population of 26 million people is at risk. Most of the country has year-round malaria transmission with a seasonal peak during the rainy season from December to April. In addition, Mozambique is prone to natural disasters such as drought, cyclones, and floods, which have likely contributed to increases in malaria transmission in recent years, particularly in low-lying coastal areas and along major rivers.

Malaria is considered the most important public health problem in Mozambique and accounts for 29% of all deaths, followed closely by AIDS at 27% (2008 Post-Census Mortality Survey). Among children less than five years old, malaria accounts for 42% of the deaths, followed by AIDS at 13%. *Plasmodium falciparum* accounts for 90% of all malaria infections, with *P. malariae* and *P. ovale* responsible for about 9% and 1%, respectively. The major vectors in Mozambique are *Anopheles gambiae* s.s., *An. arabiensis*, and *An. funestus* s.s. Of the major subspecies of the *An. gambiae* complex, *An. arabiensis* is more prevalent in the south and *An. gambiae* s.s. in the north.

The last national cross-sectional survey to measure community parasitemia prevalence was the 2011 Demographic and Health Survey (DHS). This survey showed parasitemia, diagnosed by rapid diagnostic test (RDT), varied from 1.5% in the capitol, Maputo, to 54.8% in Zambézia Province, with point prevalence higher in the northern region (varying from 43.3% to 52.1%) than in the southern region (varying from 1.5% to 36.8%). The 2011 DHS underscored the reality that malaria is a rural disease in Mozambique; prevalence in rural areas was almost three times as high as the prevalence in urban areas (46% versus 16%, respectively).

More recently, malaria cases reported through routine data collection increased from 2012 through 2014. Although reported cases increased 40% from 2013 through 2014, outpatient consultations only increased 5%, and reported deaths due to malaria increased only 10%. While the quality of these data cannot be fully validated, the fact that this increase was seen in all provinces except Maputo Province and Maputo City suggests that at least some of this increase was real. An investigation could not find any artificial explanations (increase in number of health facilities reporting, completeness of data, changes in reporting practices, etc.), and similar reports have been received for neighboring countries (Malawi, Zambia, and Zimbabwe).

3. Country health system delivery structure and Ministry of Health (MoH) organization

In Mozambique, the public sector–the National Health Service (NHS)–dominates health service delivery. Although there is a growing private sector, it is largely limited to major cities. The public sector reaches an estimated 60% of the population.

The NHS consists of four levels. Level I includes both rural and urban health centers and health posts. These health facilities provide a package of primary health care services, have very limited laboratory capacity, and usually have a maternity ward but do not provide inpatient services. According to a 2004 World Bank Report, Level I facilities represent at least 40% of all health services and are typically the first (and often only) point of contact with the health system for a large portion of the population. Level II includes district and rural hospitals that offer diagnostic, surgical, and obstetric services and have general medical doctors on their staff. Level III consists of provincial hospitals, which offer curative services, have diagnostic services/equipment, and are training centers. Finally, Level IV consists of the country's three referral hospitals in Maputo, Beira, and Nampula, serving the southern, central, and northern regions, respectively.

Recognizing the limitations of the NHS and the shortage of professionally trained health workers, the country, with United States Government (USG) support, has begun revitalizing the community health worker program, which employs health workers known as *Agentes Polivalentes Elementares da Saúde* (APEs). The APEs provide preventive and basic curative services, including malaria diagnosis (using RDTs) and treatment (with ACTs). A number of national and international non-governmental organizations also work within the NHS to assist in the provision of health services.

Malaria control in the public health system consists of three administrative levels: central, provincial, and district. At the central level, the NMCP benefits from strong leadership improving its ability to manage and coordinate programs. Each province has a provincial malaria focal point that coordinates the implementation of malaria control activities at that level. Recently, district malaria focal points were created as a way to improve data management and reporting for malaria at that level. Terms of reference for these positions have been drafted, and the positions have been advertised; the hope is that they will be filled by the end of 2015.

4. National malaria control strategy

The NMCP is responsible for developing policy, establishing norms, planning, organizing, and coordinating all malaria control activities in the country. Additional responsibilities include periodic assessment of the impact of malaria control activities, development of training materials on malaria case management for health workers at all levels, mobilization of domestic and external funds for malaria control activities, promotion of malaria awareness and advocacy, and leading operational research.

In calendar year 2012, the NMCP finalized the National Malaria Policy and the 2012-2016 National Malaria Prevention and Control Strategic Plan. The strategic plan focuses on continuing national-level scale-up of malaria prevention and control and has five objectives:

1. Decentralization of malaria control activities, with 100% of districts in 2016 having malaria management capacity in place.

2. Access to at least one prevention method for 100% of the population by 2016.

3. Confirmatory laboratory testing on 100% of suspected cases of malaria throughout the entire health system, including APEs by 2016.

4. Malaria prevention messaging reaching 100% of the population by 2016.

5. Strengthened monitoring and evaluation (M&E) system so that by 2016 all districts are capable of reporting key malaria-related indicators.

5. Updates in the strategy section

The confirmation of funding of the 2016-17 insecticide-treated net (ITN) mass distribution campaign, in addition to the discovery of pyrethroid resistance in a number of sites across the country has led the NMCP to prioritize updating the national integrated vector control strategic plan.

PMI, in line with the NMCP's strategy, recognizes the need for a concerted effort to combat malaria in the highly endemic northern provinces. The launching of a new Bill and Melinda Gates Foundation funded program in Maputo Province to gradually eliminate malaria has caused some concern about drawing resources from the north. However, while supportive of the initiative, the NMCP has clearly stated that it needs PMI resources where the malaria burden is highest.

6. Integration, collaboration, and coordination

Integrated health activities

Within the USG, the U.S. Agency for International Development (USAID) Mozambique Health Team is merged into one integrated health office, maximizing the programmatic synergies among the President's Emergency Plan for AIDS Relief (PEPFAR), PMI, and other health programs. This organizational structure encourages technical synergies and avoids duplication of efforts, as well as facilitates a broader health systems approach across all USG programs, including maternal and child health (MCH), reproductive health/family planning, tuberculosis, HIV, malaria, and nutrition. An example of integration of USAID's health projects is the Maternal and Child Survival Project (MCSP), which is jointly supported with funds from PMI, MCH, reproductive health, family planning, and PEPFAR. The project will prioritize the implementation and scale up of evidence-based, high-impact maternal, neonatal and child health (MNCH) service delivery interventions. In recognition of the prevailing causes of death and disease, the program areas to be supported under MCSP are: maternal, newborn, and child health; malaria; reproductive health and family planning; nutrition; and water, sanitation, and hygiene. HIV-related activities will be carried out on a limited basis and solely in conjuction with core MNCH and reproductive health/family planning activities. MCSP will contribute directly to one of USAID's principal global health priorities: Ending Preventable Child and Maternal Deaths and to achievement of Millenium Development Goals four, five, and six.

Other examples of PMI integrated efforts are strengthening supply chain management and supporting the rollout of the District Health Information System-2 (DHIS-2) system. PMI, PEPFAR, and family planning leverage their resources to strengthen the capacity of the Ministry of Health's (MoH's) supply chain management system through the Central Medical Stores (CMAM) and improve the supply chain at different levels. In addition, PMI and PEPFAR funds complement each other to support the development and rollout of the new DHIS-2 system, which will be a crucial step towards receiving timely, quality data on malaria indicators among others.

Collaboration and Coordination

The Global Fund's New Funding Model (NFM) concept note was written with direct input from PMI. The activities and funding were tailored so that if an activity not funded by one donor, the other supports it. An example of this distribution of activities is ITN coverage: PMI supports procurement and distribution of ITNs through ANCs for pregnant women, and Global Fund supports the procurement and distribution of the ITNs for universal coverage. PMI is providing technical support to ensure a successful implementation of the 2016/17 national ITN campaign, which will be funded through the NFM. Similarly, PMI and the Global Fund coordinate to procure all the ACTs and RDTs needed by the country. Another example of collaboration between PMI and the Global Fund is the IRS activity in Zambézia: the insecticide used in Zambézia is generally procured by the Global Fund, which allows PMI to direct its limited resources to other critical areas that the Global Fund cannot support directly, such as technical assistance.

With the expansion of the private sector in recent years, especially the extractive industries, the MoH and donors, including the USG, engaged in discussions with the private sector companies to explore the potential of public-private partnerships. However, despite some sporadic initiatives, not much progress has been achieved in establishing formal partnerships with the private sector companies. In calendar year 2014, the Brazilian mining company, Vale, donated personal protective equipment for the MoH's led IRS activities. PMI continues to recognize the potential role of private sector in supporting malaria control activities and remains committed to work with the private sector and the Government of the Republic of Mozambique (GRM) to explore the potential of public-private partnerships.

Finally, PMI has been involved in the discussions around malaria elimination activities in southern Mozambique. Currently, there are three malaria elimination initiatives focusing on southern Mozambique: two Gates-funded projects, one led by *Centro de Investigação em Saude de Manhiça* (CISM) and the other led by the Clinton Health Access Initiative; and the Malaria Elimination 8, launched by the Southern African Development Community. The Malaria Elimination 8 submitted a concept note to the Global Fund. The expectation is that these initiatives will bring additional resources to push the malaria elimination agenda in southern Mozambique, while PMI resources and most of the NFM resources will continue to be concentrated on the high burden areas of central and northern Mozambique.

7. PMI goal, objectives, strategic areas, and key indicators

Under the PMI Strategy for 2015-2020, the U.S. Government's goal is to work with PMI-supported countries and partners to further reduce malaria deaths and substantially decrease malaria morbidity, towards the long-term goal of elimination. Building upon the progress to date in PMI-supported countries, PMI will work with NMCPs and partners to accomplish the following objectives by 2020:

1. Reduce malaria mortality by one-third from 2015 levels in PMI-supported countries, achieving a greater than 80% reduction from PMI's original 2000 baseline levels.

2. Reduce malaria morbidity in PMI-supported countries by 40% from 2015 levels.

3. Assist at least five PMI-supported countries to meet the World Health Organization's (WHO) criteria for national or sub-national pre-elimination.[1]

These objectives will be accomplished by emphasizing five core areas of strategic focus:
1. Achieving and sustaining scale of proven interventions
2. Adapting to changing epidemiology and incorporating new tools
3. Improving countries' capacity to collect and use information
4. Mitigating risk against the current malaria control gains
5. Building capacity and health systems towards full country ownership

To track progress toward achieving and sustaining scale of proven interventions (area of strategic focus #1), PMI will continue to track the key indicators recommended by the Roll Back Malaria Monitoring and Evaluation Reference Group (RBM MERG) as listed below:

- Proportion of households with at least one ITN
- Proportion of households with at least one ITN for every two people
- Proportion of children under five years old who slept under an ITN the previous night
- Proportion of pregnant women who slept under an ITN the previous night
- Proportion of households in targeted districts protected by IRS
- Proportion of children under five years old with fever in the last two weeks for whom advice or treatment was sought
- Proportion of children under five with fever in the last two weeks who had a finger or heel stick
- Proportion receiving an ACT among children under five years old with fever in the last two weeks who received any antimalarial drugs
- Proportion of women who received two or more doses of IPTp for malaria during ANC visits during their last pregnancy

8. Progress on coverage/impact indicators to date

Due to the delay of the joint AIDS Indicator Survey (AIS) and Malaria Indicator Survey (MIS) from 2014 to June 2015, the most up-to-date information on key malaria indicators at the national level remains the 2011 DHS. The 2011 DHS data showed improvement in ITN coverage when compared with the 2007 MIS. Specifically, the proportion of households with at least one ITN increased from 16% in 2007 to 51% in 2011; similarly, the proportion of children under five and pregnant women who slept under an ITN the previous night increased from 7% in 2007 to 36% and 34% respectively in 2011. The proportion of women who received two or more doses of IPTp during their last pregnancy during the last two years only increased from 16% to 19%. Increasing IPTp and use of ITNs by pregnant women continues to be a challenge in Mozambique.

---

[1] http://whqlibdoc.who.int/publications/2007/9789241596084_eng.pdf

Table I: Evolution of Key Malaria Indicators in Mozambique from 2007 to 2011

Malaria Indicators*	2007 MIS (%)	2008 MICS (%)	2009 INSIDA (%)	2011 DHS (%)
Proportion of households with at least one ITN	15.8	30.7	NA	51.4
Proportion of children less than five years old who slept under an ITN the previous night	6.7	22.8	NA	35.7
Proportion of children less than five years old who slept under a bed net the previous night	15.7	42.1	48.7	38.9
Proportion of pregnant women who slept under an ITN the previous night	7.3	NA	NA	34.3
Proportion of pregnant women who slept under a bed net the previous night	19.3	NA	42.1	36.5
Proportion of women who received two or more doses of IPTp during their last pregnancy in the last two years	16.2	43.1	33.0	18.6
Proportion of children less than five years old with fever in the last two weeks who received treatment with an antimalarial within 24 hours of onset of fever	17.6	22.7	NA	22.2
Proportion of children less than five years old with fever in the last two weeks who received treatment with an ACT within 24 hours of onset of fever	4.5	NA	NA	15.3

*Years are shown as calendar years

Parasite prevalence estimates for each province, based on RDT positivity, are compared between the 2007 MIS and the 2011 DHS in Figure 1. Overall, prevalence decreased in all provinces between the two surveys, with the largest decreases occurring in Nampula (32% decrease) and Cabo Delgado (24% decrease). In total, 5 of the 11 provinces had a greater than 10% decreases in parasite prevalence between 2007 and 2011, and only three provinces had decreases less than 5%.

Figure 1. Provincial level parasite prevalence estimates, based on RDTs

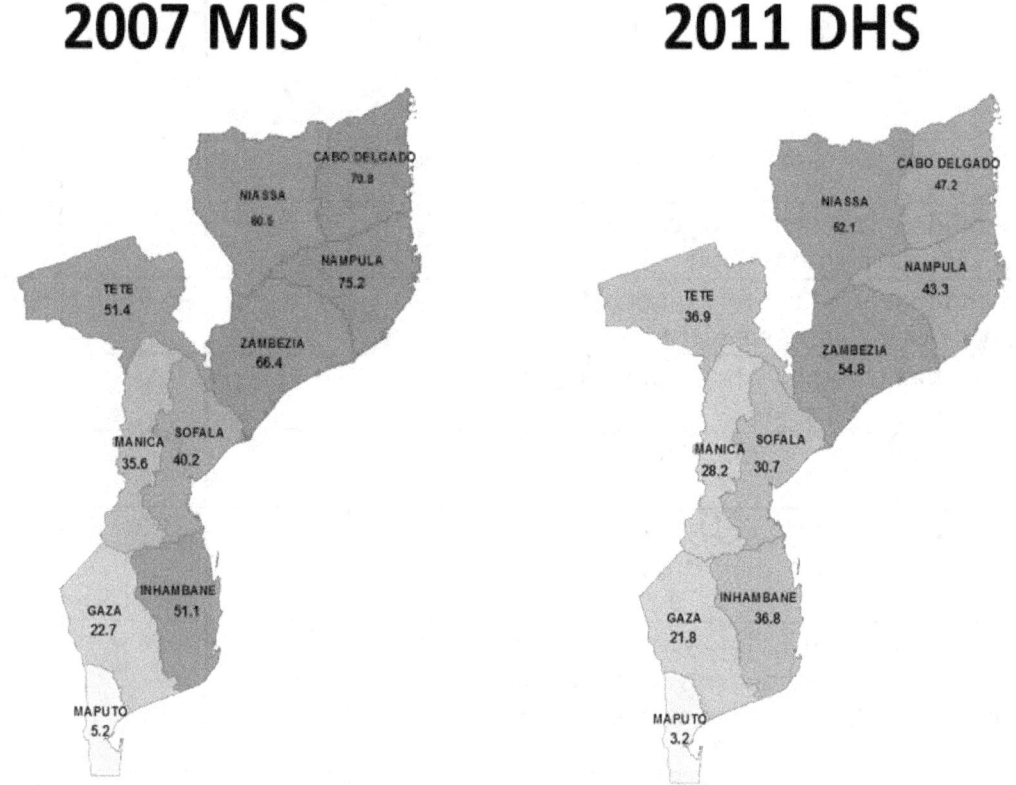

9. Other relevant evidence on progress

The results of a survey to evaluate the MoH's mass distribution campaign for ITNs in Sofala Province in calendar year 2010 demonstrated high levels of coverage of household sleeping spaces and access to ITNs (80% and 85%, respectively), which were maintained for a year after the campaign. A significant reduction in parasitemia (32%) among children under the age of five was also documented after one year. However, data from a second survey supported by PMI, conducted in Nampula Province in calendar years 2013 and 2014, indicated that one month after the campaign, only 80% and 54% of households in Nacala-a-Velha and Mecubúri Districts, respectively, received at least one net, and only 58% and 34% of households received enough ITNs to cover everyone in the household. Additionally, parasitemia in children under five years of age actually increased between 2013 and 2014, from 52% and 67%, to 61% and 87% in Nacala-a-Velha and Mecuburi, respectively. Despite the parasitemia increases in these districts, those who frequently used nets had lower estimated parasitemia prevalence than those who did not.

10. Challenges and opportunities

Challenges

The 2011 DHS results showed a slow pace of progress in scaling up malaria prevention and treatment interventions in Mozambique. In addition, routine data have shown an apparent national increase in reported cases since 2012, suggesting that prevention and treatment measures are not having the desired effect. One of the factors that may have contributed to this slow progress includes the frequent turnover of NMCP directors (six different directors in seven years), which has affected the continuity of leadership from the NMCP and MoH. In the past two years, the GRM has made significant efforts in increasing its health state budget, and the portion allocated to malaria control activities. However, most of the funding continues to come from external sources, such as the Global Fund and PMI. It is important that the GRM continues to increase its contribution to malaria control, especially to areas such as human resources development, where it is more difficult to cover with donor funding. Other challenges include shortages of appropriately educated and trained health professionals within malaria programs at the central, provincial, and district levels and high staff turnover. The comparatively massive investment in HIV programming in the country often skews budget allocation and strategic decision making throughout the country.

Three major problem areas for malaria control in Mozambique are the optimal balance between ITNs and IRS for malaria vector control (as mentioned above), the poor performance of the supply chain management system, and lack of effective behavior change communication (BCC). Supply chain issues are an ongoing challenge for all malaria commodities, but particularly for ITNs, as the country does not have a formal system for routine distribution. Leakage of commodities from the system in some provinces, particularly ITNs, has been reported. Mozambique is a large country with many remote areas and poor road conditions; many districts are not accessible during the rainy season. Information management systems to detect shortages and stockouts of malaria commodities need strengthening.

To address these challenges, PMI, in collaboration with other partners, is providing support at the central, provincial, and district levels to strengthen the supply chain and to improve M&E. In order to ensure increased accountability for ITNs procured with USG funding, PMI is supporting a temporary, semi-parallel system, for net distribution from the port of entry to the provincial level nationwide and down to the districts in target provinces. PMI recently supported the development of an insecticide resistance monitoring plan to guide vector control efforts in a coordinated, evidence-based manner.

Implementation of BCC activities is also a challenge, particularly with regard to central level policy and planning of activities. Coordination between the NMCP and the Health Promotion Department (DEPROS) is improving, and PMI has supported NMCP activities around the promotion of World Malaria Day, which were well received. More support is needed both at the central level to aid planning and development of BCC approaches and at the provincial and district levels to roll out the activities.

Opportunities

The GRM has reaffirmed its commitment to malaria prevention and control on several occasions, including during high-level visits from the Global Fund and PMI. The NMCP director, who has been in his position since March 2014, has received support from PMI, Global Fund, WHO, and others for his abilities as a leader and manager and commitment to malaria control in the country. His relationship with PMI and other partners is strong, and indications are that he will continue as director for the foreseeable future.

The updating of the Integrated Malaria Vector Control Strategy also presents a tremendous opportunity. Support from PMI and other partners for the drafting of the strategy will be of critical importance to ensure it is based on the most solid evidence, and properly addresses key issues such as resource allocation and insecticide resistance mitigation.

The approval of the national strategic plan for malaria BCC offers an opportunity to boost the implementation of BCC activities at the central, provincial, district, and community levels. PMI is leveraging the vast network of community-based organizations funded through PEPFAR and other sources to include malaria BCC messages to increase the reach of these activities.

In the past year CISM, along with the Clinton Health Access Initiative (CHAI), received funding from the Bill and Melinda Gates Foundation to begin malaria elimination activities in southern Mozambique. The goal of these investments is to eliminate malaria in Maputo Province by 2020 and use lessons learned during this exercise to scale up to the rest of the country. Although elimination is not a stated priority for the NMCP, which is focusing its efforts to high burden areas in the north of the country, this program has the potential to provide an injection of technical expertise at both central and provincial level. Moreover, provided these activities are well coordinated with existing control efforts managed through the NMCP and MoH, they have the potential to provide additional tools and insights to control malaria in Mozambique and hopefully improve the effectiveness of existing programs.

Threats

A major threat to malaria control in Mozambique is the emergence of insecticide resistance in key vector populations. Insecticide resistance to pyrethroids has now been documented in two districts in Zambezia and one in Maputo Province, forcing the switch to non-pyrethroid insecticides for IRS. As the country transitions to universal coverage of ITNs for all districts, maintaining the efficacy of these nets will be paramount. PMI will continue to support national insecticide resistance monitoring to track this issue.

Antimalarial drug resistance to artemether-lumefantrine (AL) for *P. falciparum* infections has been well documented in Southeast Asia. This may be aggravated by the problem of sub-standard drugs infiltrating the market—a growing problem in some African countries. PMI and WHO will be supporting therapeutic efficacy studies (TES) in calendar year 2015 and 2017 to monitor this issue.

III. OPERATIONAL PLAN

PMI support to Mozambique is in line with the GRM's 2012-2016 National Malaria Control Strategy. PMI funding is considered in conjunction with the other primary donor, Global Fund, as well as the NMCP and other partners, so that all resources can be allocated in an efficient and complementary manner, according to disease burden and the added value of each organization. A review of current PMI activities during the development of this operational plan found gaps in the supply chain and information systems, particularly between district and facility levels. Moreover, despite the extremely high malaria burden in the north of the country, there was no coordinated support to these provinces to improve overall performance of malaria service delivery. Based on this perspective, PMI will continue to support national level activities but will shift to more geographically focused implementation support to those provinces with the highest malaria transmission.

As a consequence of the above, PMI-supported activities will continue to focus on achieving and maintaining high coverage of ITNs nationally, particularly among the vulnerable populations of pregnant women and children under five through routine distribution systems. In addition, targeted non-pyrethroid IRS will be used to complement national universal net coverage campaigns. Service delivery activities to strengthen MIP services, improving case management, and supportive activities such as BCC, strengthening supply chain management, and M&E, will be focused primarily in high burden target provinces.

PMI commodities (ACTs, RDTs, ITNs etc.) are pooled with those purchased from other donors and distributed countrywide through the government supply chain. However, supporting interventions are implemented on a more focused geographic scale, and need to be targeted to the areas of most need. PMI began targeting support to the provinces and districts that have the highest malaria burden beginning with FY 2013 funding. The objective of this approach is to improve implementation of malaria-related activities through the facilitation of supervision, distribution of commodities, and M&E. PMI has established a provincial-level platform for BCC, MIP, M&E, and case management in three provinces (Nampula, Zambézia, and Tete) and will be establishing a fourth in Cabo Delgado. These provinces comprise approximately 55% of the country's population and support some of the highest malaria burden in Africa.

Using FY 2016 funds, and in line with MoH priorities to decentralize programming to the provincial level, PMI will focus a significant portion of its activities in these four provinces, providing consolidated support to the highest burden areas in the country. In provinces where the USG has existing partners efforts will be made to use existing mechanisms, thereby following the Global Health Initiative (GHI) mandate and avoiding duplication of efforts. Additionally, PMI will focus resources on improving the delivery and quality of care in previously underserved areas with high transmission. This support will focus on provincial and district level planning and coordination and health facility service delivery improvement.

1. Insecticide-treated nets

NMCP/PMI objectives
One of the objectives of the 2012-2016 Malaria Strategic Plan is to ensure that 100% of the population of Mozambique has access to at least one method of malaria vector control prevention

(IRS or ITNs). The Malaria Acceleration Plan 2014–2016, which is a multi-year operational plan, and Mozambique's Global Fund NFM concept note call for a scale-up of ITN distribution and a more evidence based approach for IRS. The main focus of this plan is a national, universal coverage campaign to be carried out in 2016-2017. As a result, districts that were formerly targeted to receive only IRS will now be covered by ITNs in the campaign. The Global Fund will fund the campaign, which is in the process of procuring nets for Nampula Province for 2016. The remaining funds for the 2017 campaign have been approved by the Global Fund board but are not yet available for procurement. Universal coverage of ITNs was not anticipated in the 2013 integrated vector control strategy; therefore, PMI will support the NMCP to update the country's malaria vector control strategy.

In keeping with the goals set forth in the Malaria Strategic Plan, PMI aims to:

1. Support the development and implementation of an updated integrated vector control strategy to ensure sustained ITN coverage through both routine and campaign channels;
2. Implement a temporary, semi-parallel supply chain to ensure routine distribution of ITNs to ANCs; and
3. Support post-campaign surveys to ensure successful implementation and impact of mass distribution campaigns.

Progress since PMI was launched
Mozambique introduced free distribution of ITNs to children less than five years old and pregnant women as a national policy in 2006. Since late 2009, PMI has focused its support on the purchase of ITNs for ANCs and their distribution to provincial warehouses throughout Mozambique. Although routine distribution of ITNs to pregnant women at ANC visits has been national policy since 2006, the system to support this activity has not been formalized; furthermore, PMI at present is the only donor providing funding for distribution of ITNs through routine systems. Because of weaknesses in the routine ITN logistics system, including issues with storage and logistics information, PMI is supporting a semi-parallel distribution system for routine ITNs, from port of entry to the provincial level, nationwide. The current NMCP policy for routine distribution is ANC only. In April 2013, PMI in collaboration with the NMCP organized a workshop on continuous distribution of ITNs and NetCALC, a tool used to predict ITN needs. During this workshop channels for consideration included antenatal care (ANC), Expanded Program on Immunization (EPI), schools, full-cost retail sales, and social marketing sales, and PMI was going to support pilot EPI distribution. However, the NMCP has asked PMI to focus on making sure at least one distribution system, ANC distribution, was functioning well and reliable before expanding to a second routine distribution method, given issues with stockouts of ITNs at health facilities.

In 2009, Mozambique adopted the policy of universal coverage, defined as one ITN for every two persons in ITN targeted districts the implementation of mass universal coverage campaigns started in 2010 in 11 (out of a total of 151) districts. See figure 2 for a map of ITN distributions in Mozambique from 2011 to 2015. Universal coverage campaigns were carried out in 45 districts in 2011, 21 districts in 2012, 23 districts in 2013, and 64 districts in 2014/2015. In 2014/2015, 5.2 million ITNs were distributed, completing coverage of all districts initially targeted for universal ITN distribution and beginning to cover districts that formerly received only IRS, as well as ITN replacement, which was originally scheduled for every three years.

From the 2007 MIS to the 2011 DHS, the proportion of households with at least one ITN increased from 16% to 51%. Correspondingly, the proportion of children less than five years old and pregnant women who slept under an ITN the previous night rose from 7% and 7% to 36% and 34%, respectively. A joint MIS and AIS planned for June 2015 will assess ITN coverage after the completion of mass campaigns covering all districts in Mozambique.

PMI funded a survey on the effectiveness and impact of a universal ITN distribution campaign in Nampula. The campaign took place in late 2013, and data collection ended in December 2014. The survey, jointly implemented by Field Epidemiology and Laboratory Training Program (FELTP) students, Epidemic Intelligence Service officers, and NMCP and PMI staff, showed poor net coverage in households one month following the campaign. Poor net coverage in this context was due to a lack of nets in households. Surveys in Nampula in calendar years 2013 and 2014, indicated that one month after the campaign, only 80% and 54% of households in Nacala-a-Velha and Mecubúri, respectively, received at least one net, and only 58% and 34% of households received enough ITNs to cover everyone in the household. These results point to the need for stronger, more detailed planning for future mass campaigns to ensure higher coverage. Going forward there will be more consistent planning for the nationwide mass campaign that is scheduled to begin in late 2016.

The survey also showed no significant impact of the campaign on community parasitemia, though it did show significantly lower odds of parasitemia among individuals who used nets frequently.

Figure 2: Map of Mozambique districts and years of universal ITN coverage campaigns

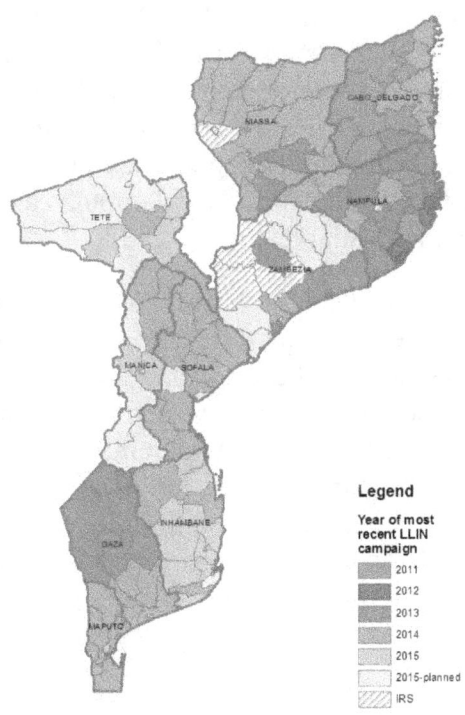

Progress during the last 12-18 months
During the past year, PMI continued to support routine distribution of ITNs to pregnant women, procuring approximately 1.4 million nets to meet the requirement for the ANC system. According to NMCP data, a total of 1,258,988 ITNs were distributed to pregnant women during calendar year 2014.

PMI continued to support a semi-parallel distribution system for ITNs, from port of entry to the provincial level, nationwide. In addition, PMI supported the distribution from port of entry directly to the districts in Cabo Delgado and Nampula Provinces, while UNICEF supported similar activities in the provinces of Zambézia, Gaza, and Tete. Despite these improvements in the distribution system, data from end-use verification (EUV) survey reports continues to show lack of consistent availability of bed nets, both at the provincial and/or district warehouse and health facility level. The last two EUV reports showed stockouts in at least 30% of warehouses visited and in about 50% of the health facilities visited. The major challenge is the delayed arrival of ITNs to the country, and in calendar year 2014, the country experienced a six-month delay from the initial planned delivery date. A similar situation is happening in the current year, and this will likely cause problems of stockouts. To overcome this challenge, the country has increased the number of ITNs to be procured, in order to create a pipeline and smooth out the supply chain.

Considerable improvements have been observed in the distribution of Global Fund-supported bed nets through mass campaigns. Although with some delays, all mass campaigns planned for 2014 were completed by May 2015, with more than 5.2 million nets distributed in 64 districts across the country. The country also made significant progress in reviewing its bed net distribution approach and has decided to implement national level campaigns, as opposed to covering selected districts across the country. The national campaign will be launched in the last quarter of calendar year 2016 in Nampula Province, and it is expected to run for approximately 12 months. All districts of the country, without exception, are therefore expected to be covered by the end of 2017. The funding to cover Nampula Province has already been secured through the Global Fund NFM mechanism, and the Global Fund is planning to support coverage for the rest of the country. The Global Fund has recently placed orders for the 2016 Nampula campaign and will order the remaining 2017 nets when funds become available.

In order to help guide the country's allocation of resources for vector control, PMI and Global Fund supported a workshop in 2014 aimed at identifying the most cost-effective mix of vector control interventions. The workshop brought together mathematical disease and economic modelers from Johns Hopkins University, the London School of Economics, and the Swiss Tropical and Public Health Institute, with the goal of helping to quantify which mix of IRS and ITNs should be targeted while writing the Global Fund NFM concept note. Initial results suggest allocating more resources to ITNs rather than IRS, and helped influence the drafting of the Global Fund concept note, which will provide the resources to cover the entire country with ITNs by the end of 2017.

Commodity gap analysis

Table II. ITN Gap Analysis

Calendar Year	2015	2016	2017
Total Targeted Population	25,727,911	26,423,623	27,128,530
Continuous Distribution Needs			
Channel #1: ANC[1]	1,385,903	1,420,662	1,456,279
Estimated Total Need for Continuous	1,385,903	1,420,662	1,456,279
Mass Distribution Needs			
2015 mass distribution campaign[2]	1,836,380		
2016/2017 mass distribution campaign[3]		3,489,047	11,510,953
Estimated Total Need for Campaigns	1,836,380	3,489,047	11,510,953
Total Calculated Need: Routine and Campaign	**3,222,283**	**4,909,709**	**12,967,232**
Partner Contributions			
ITNs carried over from previous year	0	14,097	343,435
ITNs from MoH	0	0	0
ITNs from Global Fund NFM	1,836,380	3,489,047	11,510,953
ITNs planned with PMI funding	1,400,000	1,750,000	1,130,700
Total ITNs Available	**3,236,380**	**5,253,144**	**12,985,088**
Total ITN Surplus (Gap)	**14,097**	**343,435**	**17,856**

Footnotes: [1] Based existing ANC consumption data for ITN distribution; [2] Needed to cover 3 districts in Nampula, 1 district in Inanbane, 1 in Sofala, 4 in Manica and 6 in Zambezia; [3] 2017 national universal coverage campaign will start in December 2016 in Nampula.

Plans and justification
With FY 2016 funding, PMI will support procurement and distribution of ITNs through a semi-parallel supply chain to ANC clinics nationwide. PMI will continue to support distribution of ITNs to the district level in Nampula and Cabo Delgado, with UNICEF continuing to support ANC distribution to the district level in Zambézia, Tete, and Gaza. In addition, through its provincial level support for health system strengthening in Zambezia, Tete, Nampula and Cabo Delgado, PMI will provide technical assistance and logistical planning support for provincial-health facility supply chains. ANC nets, unlike RDTs and ACTs, do not currently fall under the essential medicines system managed by CMAM, which has benefited from significant supply chain strengthening efforts by USG donors in recent years. However, there have been recent strong indications from the government that nets will be transitioned to the existing CMAM system in the near future. If this comes to fruition, PMI will provide technical assistance to support this transition and strengthen the system further as needed. In addition, PMI will help the NMCP plan for and implement the 2017 mass campaign and support a post-campaign survey to evaluate its success and guide efforts to increase usage of nets distributed. PMI will also continue to support ITN durability monitoring (see M&E section).

Proposed activities with FY 2016 funding: ($6,020,000)

- Procurement of ITNs: Approximately 1.13 million ITNs will be procured to cover the country's needs for distribution through ANC clinics. ($3,720,000)

- Support ANC distribution of ITNs: Distribution will be from port of entry to the provincial level nationwide and from port of entry to the district level in two provinces (Nampula & Cabo Delgado). Support includes transportation, warehousing, quantification of needs, and support to information systems that will allow collection of data on ITN rationing, consumption, and stock levels. ($1,900,000)

- Post-campaign survey: Currently, there are no plans by the MoH or the Global Fund to support post-campaign surveys to evaluate the effectiveness of Global Fund-funded ITN mass campaigns. Consequently, PMI will monitor the effectiveness of Mozambique's first nationwide mass ITN campaign, including household ITN coverage and the retention of campaign ITNs with a post-campaign survey occurring six months after ITN distribution in 2017. It will be important to understand how effective this campaign will be, given that results from previous campaigns showed issues with net ownership in follow-up surveys. ($300,000)

- Campaign planning and distribution technical assistance: Continued support for NMCP to plan and implement the 2017 nationwide mass ITN campaign. ($100,000)

2. Indoor residual spraying

NMCP/PMI objectives

Mozambique's 2012-2016 Malaria Strategic Plan calls for 100% of the population to have access to at least one method of malaria vector control prevention (IRS or ITNs). Mozambique's Global Fund NFM concept note and the country's Malaria Acceleration Plan 2014–2016 both call for a scale-up of ITN distribution and a more targeted approach for IRS. As a result, districts that were formerly targeted to just receive IRS are now also slated to receive universal ITN coverage. An integrated vector control strategy was drafted in 2013 that laid out criteria for selecting IRS areas (high malaria burden, high economic interest, high population but not highly urbanized centers, etc.), leading to the selection of 34 target districts nationwide. However, it did not take into account plans for universal coverage of ITNs in former IRS districts. Therefore, within the next year, with PMI support, the NMCP will be working to draft a new malaria vector control strategy that prioritizes insecticide resistance management and malaria burden reduction.

In keeping with the goals set forth in the Malaria Strategic Plan, PMI aims to:

1. Support an integrated, evidence-based approach to IRS that results in a more cost-effective and efficient targeted strategy for the entire country;
2. Support the development of an updated integrated malaria vector control strategy; and
3. Strengthen the MoH-led IRS program.

Progress since PMI was launched
PMI has supported IRS in as few as four and as many as eight districts in Zambézia since FY 2007, consistently achieving high coverage levels of above 85%. Currently, there are three groups supporting IRS in Mozambique: PMI, the MoH, and Global Fund. PMI focuses on high burden districts within Zambézia Province, and the MoH sprays the remaining target districts in the provinces outside of Zambézia. The Global Fund provides funds for insecticide procurement for both spray campaigns. However, due to the need to spray more structures than originally planned in 2014 and the switch from a pyrethroid to a long-lasting organophosphate for the 2015 campaign, PMI also procured insecticide in each of these years.

Table III: PMI-supported IRS activities 2013–2017

Calendar Year	Number of Districts Sprayed	Insecticide Used	Number of Structures Sprayed	Coverage Rate	Population Protected
2013	4	pyrethroid	414,232	89.2%	2,181,896
2014	5	pyrethroid	445,118	93.1%	2,327,815
2015*	6#	3 districts pyrethroid; 3 districts organophosphate	440,579	-	2,177,912
2016**	6	organophosphate	440,579	-	2,177,912
2017**	TBD	organophosphate	440,000	-	TBD

* Represents targets based on the draft 2015 IRS work plan.
** Represents projected targets based on national strategic plan and/or discussions with the NMCP.
# Note that Milange and Morrumbala were each split into two districts in late 2014 by the GRM.

PMI has provided a significant amount of support to build Mozambique's entomological capacity both at the central level and regionally. The PMI-supported central entomology laboratory and insectary at the National Institute of Health (INS) in Maputo is operational and serves as the reference laboratory for in-country molecular processing of mosquito material and monitoring for insecticide resistance and its mechanisms. The PMI-supported entomology laboratory and insectary in Quelimane, Zambézia Province, serves as a regional center for entomologic monitoring and surveillance for IRS and ITN activities in the central provinces of Mozambique. Similarly, PMI supported the establishment of an entomology laboratory in Pemba, Cabo Delgado Province, which serves as a regional center for entomological monitoring and surveillance in the Northern provinces.

Progress during the last 12-18 months
Because of delays in delivery of ITNs for planned 2014 mass campaigns, IRS operations in 2014 targeted five districts in Zambezia without universal ITN coverage: Mopeia, Milange,

Morrumbala, Mocuba, and Quelimane. The calendar year 2014 spray campaign, carried out from October 20 through December 13, used the pyrethroid deltamethrin. A total of 1,354 men and women were hired and trained as spray operators, team leaders, locality and district supervisors, coordinators, and warehouse keepers. Of the 477,930 structures targeted in the five districts, 445,118 were sprayed, representing 93.1% coverage of eligible structures. The total number of persons protected was 2,327,815, including 159,830 pregnant women and 404,707 children less than five years of age.

Standard WHO cone bioassays were used to evaluate the quality of the 2014 spray operation. The bioassay tests were conducted 24 hours after spraying and monthly thereafter in Mocuba, Milange, Morrumbala and Mopeia. The wall bioassay tests showed high mortality rates (100%) of susceptible mosquitoes (*Anopheles arabiensis*) exposed to deltamethrin-sprayed walls in all districts for the tests conducted 24 hours post-spray. Five months after IRS, the mortality rates were 88% and 90% for Mopeia and Milange respectively and 100% for Mocuba and Morrumbala.

Insecticide resistance testing was carried out in early 2015 in Mocuba, Milange, and Morrumbala on *An. gambiae s.l.* testing in Milange showed continued susceptibility to deltamethrin, but resistance to multiple pyrethroid insecticides was detected in both Mocuba and Morrumbala. Full susceptibility was observed to DDT, bendiocarb, and fenitrothion in Mocuba and Morrumbala.

Table IV: Insecticide Resistance Testing on *An. gambiae* s.l. in IRS Districts - 2015

District	Deltamethrin	Lambdacyhalothrin	DDT	Bendiocarb	Fenitrothion
Mocuba	74 (300)	92 (300)	100 (100)	99 (100)	100 (100)
Morrumbala	91 (300)	69 (100)	100 (100)	100 (100)	100 (100)
Milange	100 (100)	-	-	-	-

% 24-hour mortality with number tested in parentheses (>98% = susceptible, 90-97% = possible resistance, <90% = resistance)

For monitoring vector behavior, density, composition, and seasonality, five sentinel sites were selected. Four sites in the intervention districts of Mopeia, Milange, Morrumbala and Mocuba were selected, and one site, Maganja da Costa, was selected as a comparable non-intervention district. Pyrethrum spray collections and human landing catches were conducted monthly. Both methods captured *An. gambiae* s.l. and *An. funestus* s.l. In 2014, PMI also continued to collect epidemiological data at health facilities in current and former IRS districts to assess whether the number of reported malaria cases has decreased in IRS districts. Not enough data is currently available to use for decision-making purposes, but once more data are available, it will be used in conjunction with entomological data and the results of a proposed community parasitemia survey in Zambezia (*see Operational Research Section*) to refine Mozambique's vector control strategy.

In order to build NMCP entomological capacity, PMI supported the NMCP to establish entomological sentinel sites in 10 provinces (11 including Zambezia) to monitor entomology and insecticide resistance indicators and the quality and coverage of malaria vector control interventions. PMI supported sentinel sites began collecting data in 2014. Resistance data was collected from 20 sites, and suspected resistance to lambacyhalothrin, deltamethrin, and bendiocarb in *An. gambiae* s.l. was detected in the provinces of Maputo City, Maputo, and Inhambane; suspected resistance to lambacyhalothrin, deltamethrin, and bendiocarb was detected in Tete province in *An funestus*; and confirmed resistance to lambdacyhalothrin was detected in *An. funestus* in Niassa province (see tables below). In addition, PMI continued to support entomologic activities at the central and provincial levels with training, supervision, and standardization of entomology techniques. PMI recently organized a meeting with the NMCP and other partners and donors supporting entomology in order to develop a plan to decentralize many of the activities of the sentinel sites, so that the NMCP will not become overstretched. Furthermore, PMI seconded a consultant to the NMCP to provide support in the implementation and coordination of their IRS activities.

NMCP Insecticide Resistance Testing – 2014 – *An. gambiae* s.l.

Provincia	Postos Sentinela	Lambdacyhalothrin (0.05%)		Deltamethrin (0.05%)		Bendiocarb (0.01%)		DDT (4%)		Fenitrothion (1%)	
		n	% Mort.	n	% Mort.	n	% Mort.	n	% Mort.	n	% Mort.
Cabo Delgado	Metuge	200	100	100	100%	100	100	-	-	-	-
	Montepuez	150	98.7	50	100	50	98	-	-	-	-
Nampula	Ilha de Moçambique	-	-	200	100	-	-	-	-	-	-
	Meconta	200	98.5	100	100	200	100	250	98.8	-	-
Zambézia	Morrumbala			100	96	100	100	100	100	100	100
Manica	Gondola	25	100	75	100	25	100	100	100	-	-
	Chimoio	75	100	100	100	50	100	100	100	-	-
Tete	Changara	100	94	100	97	100	95	100	100	-	-
Sofala	Dondo	100	87	-	-	-	-	25	100	-	-
Inhambane	Cidade de Inhambane	100	100	100	100	100	92	100	100	-	-
Gaza	Chokwe	100	96	100	98	100	100	100	100	-	-
	Xai-Xai	100	99	100	99	100	100	100	100	-	-
Maputo Provincia	Boane	95	96.84	148	100	100	100			-	-
	Magude	97	96.97	94	100	96	100	25	100	-	-
	Moamba	97	98.97	148	100	100	100	100	100	-	-
Cidade de Maputo	Distrito Urbano Ka Maxaquene	144	90.3	97	81.4	85	81.2	100	100	-	-
	Total	1583		1562		1306		1200		100	

NMCP Insecticide Resistance Testing – 2014 – *An. funestus* s.l.

Provincia	Posto	Lambdacyhalothrin (0.05%)		Deltamethrin (0.05%)		Bendiocarb (0.01%)		DDT (4%)		Fenitrothion (1%)	
		n	% Mort.	n	% Mort.	n	% Mort.	n	% Mort.	n	% Mort.
Niassa	Lichinga	100	87	100	100	-	-	-	-	-	
Zambézia	Mocuba	100	100	100	100	100	100	100	100	100	100
	Milange	-	-	50	100	-	-			-	-
Tete	Moatize	125	93	125	95	125	91	125	99	-	-
	Total	325		375		225		225		100	

Plans and justification

Mopeia will be covered with ITNs before the 2015 rainy season, but the other PMI-supported IRS districts will not receive universal ITN coverage until the 2017 nationwide mass campaign. Because of the detection of pyrethroid resistance in Morrumbala and Mocuba, PMI will support IRS with a long-lasting organophosphate in those districts in 2015, as well as in Derre, the new district recently split off from Morrumbala. PMI will continue to support IRS with a pyrethroid insecticide in Quelimane, Milange, and Molumbo, the new district recently split off from Milange. PMI will procure enough long-lasting organophosphate to cover 254,781 structures.

For 2016, Global Fund will be purchasing enough long-lasting organophosphate to cover all six IRS districts in Zambezia. Mozambique has been included as a first round country in a UNITAID proposal for a market intervention to accelerate the uptake of long-lasting, non-pyrethroid IRS, which will mean that Mozambique will be eligible to buy subsidized long-lasting organophosphate starting in 2016. By the start of the 2017 spray season in October, all districts in Zambezia are expected to be covered with ITNs. Therefore, PMI will conduct IRS with a non-pyrethroid insecticide in targeted districts based on criteria to be laid out in the revision of the NMCP vector control strategy, including status of insecticide resistance, malaria burden, and population density. Although current IRS efforts are focused in only Zambezia province, the review of the national integrated vector control strategy may necessitate a change in geographic scope but PMI will maintain coverage of up to 440,000 structures.

Epidemiologic and entomologic surveillance will be undertaken in current and former IRS districts. Entomological monitoring will be done monthly and include assessment of vector behavior, density, composition, seasonality, and insecticide resistance. Epidemiologic monitoring will be based on extracting data from health facility records or, if in place, the DHIS-2 system. The epidemiologic surveillance data will be used for 1) measuring the impact of the IRS campaigns, with the hope that the data will inform future decisions regarding vector control in the country, and 2) detecting any increase in cases at HFs that may signal a failure of vector control. If an increase is detected this will trigger an investigation and potentially further control measures, based on an epidemic response plan that is currently being drafted. PMI will also provide support to the MoH in their national IRS program in PMI's target provinces by conducting an IRS training of trainers in a cascade approach for the central level NMCP team, provincial malaria managers, and key malaria staff. PMI will provide support for the supervision of the MoH-led national campaign to help improve the quality of spray operations, as well as limited support to environmental compliance-related activities. This national technical assistance has been included in the 2015 Mozambique Supplemental Environmental Assessment.

The NMCP's National Entomology Monitoring and Evaluation Plan for 2012–2016 includes insecticide resistance and residual efficacy testing for the IRS and ITN programs and vector bionomics at sentinel entomologic sites. The number of entomologic sentinel sites and activities will be maintained in 2016 and 2017.

Proposed activities with FY 2016 funding: ($6,959,000)

- IRS implementation: Support IRS operations covering approximately 440,000 structures. PMI-supported activities will include purchasing equipment and supplies, training, supervision, and monitoring of health facility data in current and former IRS districts. ($6,000,000)

- Entomological monitoring: Support ongoing entomologic monitoring activities in the PMI IRS districts. In addition, PMI will support MoH vector control activities, including expanded entomological monitoring nationwide in as many as 20 sentinel sites (two in each province outside of Zambezia) and processing of samples. ($500,000)

- Support to national government IRS program: Support for training of trainers through a cascade approach, supervision of IRS activities, and environmental compliance activities. ($400,000)

- IRS environmental assessment: Support independent environmental monitoring of IRS program: recommended every two years. ($30,000)

- Entomological TA: Provide entomological technical assistance through two TDYs. ($29,000)

3. Malaria in pregnancy

NMCP/PMI objectives
Prevention of malaria in pregnant women, through the use of sulfadoxine-pyrimethamine (SP) for IPTp and ITN distribution, has been promoted in Mozambique since 2006. The country has recently adopted the WHO guidelines on IPTp, which recommend monthly doses of SP during pregnancy at the beginning of the second trimester. The national guidelines also recommend supplementation with iron and folic acid during pregnancy; the available tablets in Mozambique contain 90 mg of ferrous sulfate and 1 mg of folic acid. Recommended treatment of malaria during pregnancy is with oral quinine in the first trimester and ACTs in the second and third trimesters. Although procurement of SP and ITNs for distribution through ANCs is supported by the NMCP and its partners, the implementation of MCH programs is managed by the MoH's MCH department. Both entities have identified focal persons for MIP and these individuals work very closely together. The priority for the MoH MCH program is the implementation of an

"Integrated Reproductive Health/Maternal-Neonatal-Child Services Package." A key objective of both the NMCP and the MCH Department is to ensure that 85% of women who have completed a pregnancy in the last two years will have received two or more doses of IPTp during that pregnancy.

In alignment with GRM objectives, PMI aims to achieve the following objectives:

> 1. Ensure point-of-care delivery of MCH services through provincial and district support of supervision and training of ANC health workers.

> 2. Support simplification of the delivery and reporting of SP uptake by pregnant women through ensuring widespread adoption of the WHO guidelines and training in their implementation.

Progress since PMI was launched
IPTp coverage in Mozambique has remained almost stagnant over the past eight years. The percentage of women who receive at least two doses of SP during pregnancy increased slightly from 16% in 2007 (2007 MIS) to 19% in 2011 (2011 DHS). The MoH is paying considerable attention to improve the coverage of this indicator. The primary vehicle for delivering this support has been the "Integrated Reproductive Health/Maternal-Neonatal-Child Services Package," which was launched in 2012. PMI has contributed to this effort, along with other USAID funding sources, since FY 2009. The USG has supported the development of national policies, norms, and guidelines; conducted training on the integrated in-service training package; provided support for the improvement of the quality of care; provided input in the revision of the MCH registers to enable better recording and reporting practices; and coordinated MCH partners under the leadership of the MoH. As a result of this effort, the routine data is showing an improvement of IPTp coverage nationally from 20% in 2011 to 36% in 2013 to 44% in 2014, and an even greater improvement in PMI-supported facilities.

The reasons for the low coverage of IPTp are complex, but are thought to result primarily from lack of supervision at ANC facilities, poor performance of the supply chain with national stockouts of SP, and lack of clearly articulated guidelines on the administration of IPTp. In addition, it is thought that a high percentage of women that receive both IPTp and ITNs are not recorded, making the coverage of these interventions artificially low and emphasizing the need for better monitoring and reporting of MIP indicators at the health facility level. In the past several years, the MCH department at the MoH has undergone an internal reorganization, and changes in personnel have resulted in increased collaboration with the NMCP.

Progress during the last 12-18 months
PMI continued its support for the rollout of the new WHO IPTp guidelines. During FY 2014, the support included the revision of the ANC registers and the update of several materials such as the Flowchart Book for Reproductive, Maternal and Newborn Care; the Integrated In-service Training Packages for Reproductive Maternal Newborn and Child Health, including the Newborn and Malaria in Pregnancy module; and other training materials. Since June 2014, the new guidelines have been implemented nationwide.

To support the supply of SP, approximately 8.2 million tablets of SP were purchased in 2014 with USG funds. This amount was supplemented with 6 million tablets procured by the GRM and 4.5 million tablets through UNICEF. Despite this effort, the data from the last EUV report (Q1 2015) showed the occurrence of stockouts in 20% of the health facilities visited. No stockouts were reported at the warehouse level, suggesting that management issues, rather than availability of the drug in the district may cause the stockouts at health facility.

PMI has continued to support provision of ANC services to pregnant women through training and supervision. PMI support focused on 108 health facilities involved in the Model Maternities Initiative, a MoH-led effort to roll out a package of priority interventions to target the drivers of maternal and neonatal mortality. Data from the health facilities receiving USAID and PMI support in the context of the Model Maternity Initiative indicate that, in the first quarter of 2015, 70,098 pregnant women attended the first ANC visit, and 34% of these women attended the four ANC visits recommended by national guidelines; 53% received at least two doses of IPTp and 29% received at least three doses. There was a significant increase in the proportion of pregnant women receiving a bed net, from 75% in 2014 to 81% in the first quarter of 2015.

In terms of training and supervision, PMI supported the training of 158 health workers in IPTp. PMI also supported the School of Medicine of the Eduardo Mondlane University and the Maputo Nurse Institute's inclusion of IPTp in their pre-service training curricula. This was a part of a two-week course designed to help lecturers improve their clinical teaching competencies in the area of MNCH/RH/FP. As a result, 12 lecturers and 31 recent graduates were trained. Regular supervision visits were carried out in the 108 model maternities and in selected health facilities of Zambézia and Nampula provinces. In the first quarter of the current fiscal year, 97 supervision visits were carried out in Zambézia and 27 were carried out in Nampula.

A recent PMI supported BCC pilot intervention contributed to increasing the uptake of IPTp by promoting early attendance of ANC services, increasing awareness of pregnant women to the dangers of malaria and the benefits of IPTp, and by addressing some of the cultural norms and beliefs that may act as barriers for IPTp uptake. Such experiences are crucial to guiding future implementation of BCC activities around MIP in Mozambique.

Commodity gap analysis

Table V. SP Gap Analysis for Malaria in Pregnancy

Calendar Year	2015	2016	2017
Total Population	25,718,054	26,412,441	27,125,576
SP Needs			
Total number of pregnant women attending ANC	1,170,620	1,202,275	1,234,348
Total SP Need (in treatments)	**1,791,049**	**1,935,663**	**2,086,048**
Partner Contributions			
SP carried over (deficit) from previous year	*891,636*	*5,325,295*	*3,389,633*
SP from MOH	*1,991,375*	*0*	*260,951*
SP from Global Fund	0	0	0
SP from Other Donors (UNICEF)	1,500,000	0	0
SP planned with PMI funding	2,733,333	0	0
Total SP Available	**7,116,344**	**5,325,295**	**3,650,584**
Total SP Surplus (Gap)	**5,325,295**	**3,389,633**	**1,564,536**
Needed pipeline: 9 months (should be ≤ total SP surplus)	**1,343,287**	**1,451,747**	**1,564,536**

Footnotes: The national SP needs are calculated based on the following assumptions: 1) The estimated number of pregnant women is calculated as 5% of overall population, adjusted for the ANC attendance trends (91% coming for at least 1 visit; Mozambique DHS 2011 report) and; 2)The estimated treatments needed are calculated with the consideration of the current ANC visit attendance and current IPTp provision given the supply chain constrains and other limiting factors, adjusted for the desired yearly improvement in IPTp uptake. The estimated total SP needs are calculated in treatments (3 tablets each treatment).

The surplus in the SP tablets purchased is due to the delay in UNICEF funding, resulting in the GRM and PMI covering the SP needs early in the year, with the planned UNICEF SP supplies received later in the year. The SP stocks have expiration dates up to 2019. Therefore, no further purchases of SP in 2016 and 2017 are currently planned (other than MOH to ensure sufficient pipeline in 2017), pending adjustments/revisions based on the actual consumption.

Plans and justification

With FY 2016 funding, PMI plans to expand MIP activities to all districts in the four target provinces of Zambézia, Nampula, Tete, and Cabo Delgado. PMI will support mentoring, supervision, and training to ANC staff to provide a comprehensive package of malaria interventions (case management, IPTp, and ITNs) to pregnant women. In addition, there will be additional focus on the collection and reporting of key MIP indicators. BCC related to MIP will also be implemented at both the provincial level in these target provinces, as well as limited national-level support.

PMI will continue to provide central level support for MIP policy and planning, particularly to the integrated supervision of health workers at ANCs. In additional, PMI will work on revitalizing the national MIP working group and support the NMCP and ANC MIP focal persons. The rollout of the new WHO IPTp guidelines is now complete and the focus is now shifting to ensure compliance at facilities. PMI will continue to support the supervision and training of the ANC health workers to ensure proper and consistent implementation of the WHO guidelines, and the rollout of ANC registers that will collect malaria-specific indicators. Of note is that the GRM has continuously increased their contribution to fulfilling the SP needs in the country and are committed to fulfill all SP needs in the country during the next several years.

PMI support to strengthen M&E at national, provincial and district levels includes MIP activities, primarily through supporting the MoH's DHIS-2 system and updating reporting forms to record IPTp delivery according to the new policy, training staff on the reporting forms and integrating MIP data into district and provincial level decision-making.

Proposed activities with FY 2016 funding: ($750,000)

- Support national MIP planning and implementation: Central level technical assistance for updating of policies, training and supervision materials for MIP. ($250,000)

- ANC Training and supervision: Provincial-level support for training and supervision of ANC staff in MIP. Decentralized support for integrated in-service training and supervision of ANC health workers on MIP, particularly for the WHO IPTp policy implementation, in all districts of four targeted provinces (Cabo Delgado, Nampula, Zambézia, and Tete), with additional support for training and supervision provided as part of the integrated health package through activities and funds described in the M&E and HHS sections. ($500,000)

4. Case management

a. Diagnosis and Treatment

NMCP/PMI objectives
According to Mozambique's national treatment guidelines, all patients suspected of having malaria must have a confirmatory diagnostic test before receiving treatment with an ACT. Due to difficulties involved in implementing and ensuring the presence of high-quality microscopy, RDTs are the preferred test for primary diagnosis of malaria outside of provincial level reference hospitals and were rolled out nationally in 2011. Microscopy is reserved for suspected treatment failures, severe febrile illness, and cases referred from lower levels of care. The NMCP and PMI prioritize the scaling up of quality-assured diagnostic testing through procurement of microscopes, laboratory supplies, reagents, and RDTs; supporting training and supportive supervision; and scaling up quality assurance systems for malaria diagnostics.

In line with the GRM objectives, PMI aims to achieve the following objectives:
1. Expand and strengthen supervision and training of malaria case management at the provincial level and below through the implementation of provincial focal points for malaria case management
2. Improve the forecasting, allocation, distribution, stock management, and use of case management commodities (i.e., ACTs and RDTs) in the country

3. Implement a quality control/quality assurance program for both microscopy and RDTs

Mozambique's national guidelines for malaria treatment were last updated in 2011. Artemether-lumefantrine (AL) remains the first-line treatment for uncomplicated malaria, and artesunate-amodiaquine is the recommended alternative antimalarial. Quinine is the recommended treatment for pregnant women during their first trimester, as AL is not recommended by WHO in this population. Rectal artesunate is recommended for pre-referral treatment of severe malaria and is starting to be rolled out. Parenteral artesunate is the recommended treatment for severe malaria.

The NHS covers approximately 60% of the population. In 2011, Mozambique launched a revitalization of the APE program with the intent that this cadre of trained health workers would extend the reach of the NHS and provide health-related care to the remaining 40% of the population. Currently, APEs provide 80% and 20% of rural communities' preventive and curative care, respectively, for illnesses such as upper respiratory tract infections, diarrheal diseases, and malaria. APEs serve as the first-line of defense against malaria for people living in rural Mozambique and are trained to diagnose malaria with RDTs and provide ACTs to those with positive test results. The APE program is an important component of Mozambique's malaria case management plan and, for many residents, is the only option for appropriate malaria diagnosis and treatment.

In 2013, the GRM decided to decentralize its approach to health care and prevention, a plan now being implemented. While previously many of the health-related responsibilities, including oversight and training of health care workers, behavioral communication, and distribution of commodities were managed at the central level, they now fall under the purview of the provincial governments. Despite this shift, the goal of the NMCP remains to ensure the entire population of the country has access to proper malaria diagnostics and treatment.

Progress since PMI was launched
In support of the NMCP objectives, the National Reference Laboratory for Blood Parasites was refurbished, quality assurance testing practices were developed, and supervision guidelines for malaria diagnosis were completed. In addition, central and regional level training of microscopy trainers was performed, followed by the subsequent training of 95% of the existing laboratory staff in the country by these trainers.

PMI has historically supported the procurement of laboratory consumables used for quality control activities and training of staff. PMI supported the training of eight reference laboratory staff on malaria microscopy, including slide preparation, slide reading, parasite density measurements, and standard operating procedures. The training was carried out at CISM, which has a laboratory with International Organization for Standardization certification for malaria.

PMI has historically procured at least one third of the nation's annual RDT needs to support the provision of appropriate case management, although the roll out of RDTs continues to face several challenges, including limited consumption data and distribution plans, poor warehousing and storage practices, and poor logistics management. Stockouts continue to occur at the peripheral (health facility) level, although stocks at the district and provincial level have been improving. Due to the lack of quality data on consumption and performance of RDTs, forecasting efforts have been hampered, which in turn affect stocks of commodities at all levels.

Since 2007, significant progress has been made to simplify and streamline national standards of care for malaria treatment. In 2011, national case management guidelines were finalized in line with WHO treatment guidelines for uncomplicated and severe malaria. Clinicians at all levels of the health system have been trained on the implementation of these guidelines in all 11 provinces. Support for these programs has historically been provided at the central level, but with the policy shift towards decentralization, there is now a larger emphasis on building capacity at the provincial, district, and health facility levels.

The most recent completed therapeutic efficacy study (TES) of ACTs was carried out in 2011 and showed a 28-day polymerase chain reaction corrected efficacy for AL of 96.0% and for artesunate-amodiaquine of 99.6%[2]. For 2015, WHO is sponsoring a TES in the provinces of Cabo Delgado, Sofola, Tete, and Gaza. Genotyping to evaluate for the k13 mutation associated with artemisinin resistance will be performed by a collaborating center of WHO.

Progress during the last 12-18 months
PMI and the Global Fund together continue to purchase all RDTs and ACT treatments needed in Mozambique each year. After discovering a significant surplus of commodities during the FY 2015 MOP, amounts of commodities to be purchased with FY 2014 and FY 2015 funds were corrected to adjust the pipeline to more appropriate levels. Although quantification of ACTs and RDTs has improved in the past year, much work still needs to be done to improve the quality of consumption data. Similarly, a study done last year showed poor performance of clinicians with regards to RDT use, with 78% of patients included in the study being asked about the presence of fever and only 13% of clinicians following the proper procedures for administering and reading RDTs. To better understand diagnosis and treatment behaviors, a health facility survey is planned in mid-2015, which is expected to provide key information on case management practices and commodity consumption.

In previous years, the procurement of parenteral artesunate for the treatment of severe malaria was covered by PROSAUDE (Mozambique's Common Fund of Support for the Health Sector), donors, and the Global Fund. Funding has been allocated to cover future needs through the Global Fund NFM.

PMI has worked with partners to support warehousing and drug management at the central and provincial levels. Stockout data from the EUVs carried out in Zambézia, Nampula, Manica, Gaza, Maputo, Sofala, and Tete Provinces between January and April of 2014 were encouraging. None of the 25 health facilities were found to have complete AL stockouts at the time of the EUV visits. However, although 91% of the provincial warehouses had two or more presentations

---

[2] Nhama, A., Q. Bassat, S. Enosse, A. Nhacolo, R. Mutemba, E. Carvalho, E. Naueia, E. Sevene, C. Guinovart, M. Warsame, S. Sanz, A. Mussa, G. Matsinhe, P. Alonso, A. Tiago and E. Macete (2014). "In vivo efficacy of artemether-lumefantrine and artesunate-amodiaquine for the treatment of uncomplicated falciparum malaria in children: a multisite, open-label, two-cohort, clinical trial in Mozambique." Malar J **13**: 309.

of AL, 9% were without any AL. Additionally, only 50% of the health facilities and only 62% of the warehouses had appropriate storage conditions for AL. Of the malaria case records reviewed during the EUVs, 100% of children under five were treated appropriately with AL, while 97% of people older than five years were treated appropriately with an ACT.

PMI has continued to focus the majority of its case management efforts at the provincial level and below. In the past 12 months, malaria diagnostic refresher trainings, clinical and laboratory training of trainers, RDT quality assurance and refresher courses, covering a total of 185 central, provincial, and district laboratory and clinical staff, have occurred in Nampula and Zambezia. Two rounds of outreach training and support supervision visits have also taken place in Nampula, reaching a total of 37 health facilities in 19 districts and will start in Zambezia in the coming months. FY 2015 funds will be used to continue these activities in Zambezia and Nampula, as well as to expand into Tete and Cabo Delgado provinces.

The APE program has been progressively scaled up since calendar year 2011. Since the process began, 3,056 new APEs have been trained and 3,041 are currently working across the 11 provinces of Mozambique. The MoH, USAID, and other donors continue to discuss the necessary number of APEs needed to provide sufficient coverage for the rural areas that extend beyond the reach of the NHS. Partners, including Village Reach and UNICEF, are gathering critical data from APEs on malaria treatment, diagnosis, and commodity usage. Specifically, preliminary UNICEF data from calendar year 2013 showed that 84% of APEs reported consultation data, and performed 804,979 consultations. APEs identified 354,327 cases of malaria, 84.5% of which were confirmed with RDT and 89.7% received an antimalarial treatment. Children under five years of age represented 52.3% of the cases of malaria diagnosed by APEs. Although PMI did not support the training of APEs, PMI has provided central level support to continue the expansion and training of APEs throughout the country, and all of the RDTs and ACTs used in this program are purchased by either PMI or the Global Fund.

Commodity gap analysis

Table VI: RDT Gap Analysis

Calendar Year	2015	2016	2017
RDT Needs			
Target population at risk for malaria[#]	25,727,911	26,423,623	27,128,530
Total number projected fever cases*	24,441,515	25,102,442	25,772,104
Percent of fever cases confirmed with microscopy	15%	15%	15%
Percent of fever cases confirmed with RDT	85%	85%	85%
Total RDT Needs[£]	**32,894,206[£]**	**21,337,076**	**21,906,288**
Partner Contributions			
RDTs carried over (deficit) from previous year	22,304,925	2,731,365	592,690
RDTs from MoH	0	0	0
RDTs from Global Fund	6,070,646	11,198,401	13,330,673
RDTs from Other Donors	0	0	0
RDTs planned with PMI funding	7,250,000	8,000,000	9,000,000
Total RDTs Available	**35,625,571**	**21,929,766**	**22,923,363**
Total RDT Surplus (Gap)	**2,731,365**	**592,690**	**1,017,075**

[#] Estimates for the entire population of the country; obtained from forecasting provided by the GRM

*Calculated with the assumption, obtained from country quantification exercises, that 0.95 febrile episodes per person per year will seek care.

[£] The 2015 RDT needs includes a 7-month pipeline supply

Table VII: ACT Gap Analysis

Calendar Year	2015	2016	2017
ACT Needs			
Target population at risk for malaria[#]	25,727,911	26,423,623	27,128,530
Total projected number of malaria cases[*]	11,935,924	11,936,088	11,923,306
Total ACT Needs[¥]	**17,953,619[£]**	**11,339,283**	**11,327,140**
Partner Contributions			
ACTs carried over (deficit) from previous year	8,063,573	3,226,099	200,710
ACTs from MoH	0	0	0
ACTs from Global Fund	6,330,575	5,465,894	6,135,722
ACTs from Other Donors	0	0	0
ACTs planned with PMI funding	6,785,570	2,848,000	5,000,000
Total ACTs Available	**21,179,718**	**11,539,993**	**17,950,923**
Total ACT Surplus (Gap)	**3,226,099**	**200,710**	**9,292**

[#] Population estimates for the entire country; obtained from forecasting provided by the GRM
[*] Assumes a progressive decrease in malaria cases per person due to interventions (5% in 2015, 7.5% in 2016, and 10% in 2017, all compared with the 2014 rate of 0.4883 malaria cases per person per year)
[¥] Assumes 5% of the target population will receive a non-ACT for malaria treatment (e.g., first trimester of pregnancy, intolerance, etc.).
[£] The 2015 ACT needs includes a 7-month pipeline supply

Plans and justification

PMI and the Global Fund will continue to supply the vast majority of the case management commodities for the country, including all the RDTs and ACTs to meet the needs of the country and provide a seven-month buffer; these commodities will be distributed to all levels of the health system, including to district health facilities and APEs. Severe malaria treatment (parenteral and rectal artesunate) will be funded by the GRM and Global Fund. Although data from the last two years indicate a possible upsurge in malaria cases, much speculation surrounds the methods used to collect this data as well as the final numbers themselves. More accurate case counts from early 2015 indicate that numbers are decreasing, and we have projected this trend into the future.

PMI will work to provide more concerted support to supervision at the provincial, district and facility level. This support will be focused in Tete, Zambezia, Nampula and Cabo Delgado, the four high burden provinces in the north of the country. Support will focus on improving supervisory capacity at the provincial level, while also strengthening the capacity of districts to supervise facilities and manage quality issues more effectively.

Consistent with WHO recommendations regarding therapeutic monitoring of ACTs, Global Fund aims to sponsor a TES scheduled to commence two years after the ongoing WHO-sponsored

TES, incorporating the same sites and possibly including new ones (e.g., Manhica). PMI will continue to coordinate with these organizations and offer assistance, such as k13 resistance testing, if needed.

PMI will continue to strengthen the INS capacity at the central level to implement quality assurance activities for malaria microscopy and RDTs. This support will primarily ensure the quality assurance/quality control (QA/QC) system is functional, through support of shipment of samples to and from provinces, and procurement of materials necessary to support the system. It will primarily be used to increase the number of facilities currently participating in the QA/QC system and also build the capacity of central level supervisors through expert-level microscopy trainings. These individuals will be supported to undertake provincial supervisions.

PMI will also continue its decentralized support through supervision of malaria diagnosis and case management activities at the provincial level in four targeted provinces (Tete, Cabo Delgado, Zambezia, and Nampula). District health facility and community level supervision will also be continued. In addition, periodic refresher trainings on microscopy and RDT use will take place for laboratorians and supervisors in these provinces.

Proposed activities with FY 2016 funding: ($9,110,000)

- Procure ACTs: PMI will procure approximately 5 million ACTs (AL) for the treatment of uncomplicated malaria. ($4,950,000)

- Procure RDTs: PMI will procure approximately 9 million single species RDTs. ($2,700,000)

- Provincial, district, and health center level laboratory support and training: Provide supervision of laboratory staff in malaria laboratory diagnosis, use of RDTs, and quality assurance. ($700,000)

- Central level laboratory support: Support the INS Reference Laboratory with the rollout and scale up of the national quality assurance/quality control system, building of central level laboratory capacity, and continue supervisory visits for malaria case management from the central to provincial level. ($250,000)

- Continuation of provincial level training: Continued support to improve supervisory capacity for malaria case management in Cabo Delgado and Tete as well as transitioning ownership of this activity in the provinces of Nampula and Zambezia. ($500,000)

- Laboratory strengthening technical assistance: Support of laboratory strengthening activities to NMCP and quality control support. ($10,000)

b. Pharmaceutical Management

NMCP/PMI objectives

Both the MoH and its partners have recognized the need to strengthen the MoH's supply chain system, in order to support service delivery. CMAM is the national entity with primary responsibility within the MoH for all central-level supply chain functions, including procurement of all pharmaceuticals and related health supplies. In collaboration with the NMCP, CMAM continues to manage forecasting needs and supervises the procurement, storage, and distribution of all malaria commodities, except ITNs, from the central level to the provincial warehouses.

Malaria medicines and RDTs are delivered through two parallel CMAM logistical systems, one known as the kit system and a second known as the *Via Clássica*. The kit system is supported by PMI and it was developed in response to the bulky ACT packaging, which makes it difficult to fit in the essential medicine kit. Currently, PMI supports this system, which runs together with the essential medicines kit. These malaria kits are distributed to both health facilities and APEs through a push system.

The second logistics system, the *Via Clássica*, distributes medicines and RDTs on a quarterly basis. The products are delivered to warehouses in Maputo, Beira and Nacala, which in turn supply the three existing central hospitals and ten provincial warehouses. Each of the ten provincial warehouses supply the district warehouses, rural hospitals, general hospitals, and provincial hospitals. Malaria drugs, including AL, are managed within this system, which requires health facilities to report consumption data and place orders for commodities.

Despite these two systems, stockouts are still common with facilities often having to wait for the next kit to arrive with replenishments rather than placing orders through the *Via Clássica*. Moreover, there is little use of consumption or stock level data at the provincial or district levels, meaning supervisors and managers cannot help facilities manage their stocks. One consequence of this breakdown is that facilities will often use APE kits (stored at the facility) to fill gaps in their own supplies, thus causing stockouts at the community level.

In alignment with the GRM, PMI aims to achieve the following objectives:

1. Develop more effective public sector medical supplies/commodity procurement capacity.

2. Improve public sector warehousing and distribution at all levels.

3. Improve the use of medicines and develop more effective pharmaceutical services.

4. Strengthen the MoH/Pharmacy Department's strategic planning and management capacity.

5. Strengthen overall regulatory capacity.

Progress since PMI was launched

The USG has made significant contributions toward supply chain strengthening and improvement of pharmaceutical management in efforts to support access to good quality commodities. The USG has been the major partner providing technical assistance to CMAM. Most of the support has been provided through PEPFAR. PMI funds have complemented PEPFAR resources to strengthen central-level warehousing by refurbishing the main central warehouse, Zimpeto, located in the outskirts of Maputo, and the Beira regional warehouse in Sofala Province. Together with another Maputo-based warehousing complex, Adil, these warehouses are linked to the Beira warehouse to form a centrally managed, national system with accurate information on stock status for all essential commodities. The Nampula regional warehouse will also be linked to this system in the coming months.

PMI supported the introduction and roll out of ACTs and RDTs on a national level and the development of a supply chain master plan. Despite the problems with Mozambique's pharmaceutical management and supply chain system, data from the EUV indicates that ACTs and RDTs are reaching the health facilities in all 11 provinces of the country.

Through significant efforts on the part of CMAM, the NMCP, and USG donors, a computerized Logistics Management and Information System (LMIS) is now operational nationally in all provincial capitals and in 68 out of 151 districts. This computer-based, real-time LMIS, called *Sistema de Informação de Medicamentos e Artigos Médicos* (SIMAM), is an Access-based program and relatively easy to use. Warehouse staff in all provinces has been trained in the use of this program. The plan is to continue the roll out of the SIMAM system to all districts with USG and Global Fund support. The impact of the roll out of the SIMAM system is now visible. The proportion of districts reporting consumption of ACTs and RDTs has increased considerably from 17% in calendar year 2012 to 93% in calendar year 2014. In terms of product distributed, 67% of what was distributed in calendar year 2013/2014 was reported as consumed. In spite of these improvements in the reporting rates, additional work is needed to ensure that all health facilities within a given district report consistently.

PMI also started the process of decentralizing its support to districts, by placing a logistic advisor in Zambézia Province. These advisors will work closely with the provincial and district authorities to ensure that health facilities report consumption data routinely and experience fewer stockouts.

Progress in the past 12-18 months

During the past year, PMI continued to provide support to CMAM through provision of technical assistance, procurement of commodities and support to the ACT and RDT kitting system. PMI also continued to support supervision of health facilities through the implementation of the EUV tool and supporting supply chain management supervision. Stock taking for all malaria products was carried out in 106 health facilities.

PMI continued its support to the Malaria Case Management Working Group, which was established several years ago through a collaborative effort of various USG implementing partners and other donors. This working group supports the management and oversight of health commodities through the regular update of the quarterly supply plans, besides other duties. This working group is also responsible for coordinating quantifications and gap analyses, and to track consumption data of malaria commodities. In 2014, 93% of districts reported consumption of ACTs and RDTs and 63% of what was distributed was reported as consumed. In spite of these improvements in the reporting rates, additional work is needed to ensure that all health facilities and APEs within a given district report consistently.

In order to improve the management of the supply chain, over the past 12 months PMI continued to decentralize its support to the districts. Additional logistic advisors were placed in target provinces. Currently, there are 7 logistic advisors who provide support to 10 of the 11 provinces as follows: one regional advisor for Nampula and Niassa; one regional advisor for Sofala and Manica; one provincial advisor for Cabo Delgado; and one for Zambézia. In addition, there are three advisors based in Maputo who provide support to Maputo, Gaza, Inhambane and Tete Provinces. These advisors work closely with the provincial and district authorities to improve supply chain management and ensure health facilities report consumption data routinely. Their support focuses on strengthening supervision and training of health staff and implementation of quarterly meetings.

Other activities implemented in the past year include preparation and dissemination of monthly stock on hand reports, printing of manuals and forms, and rental payments at the main warehouse in Maputo. In addition, PMI continued to support the preparation and transport of ACT and RDT kits. It is estimated that in the past year, almost three million ACTs and 6 million RDTs were distributed to APEs and health facilities through the kit system.

Plans and justification
With the anticipated reduction of PEPFAR contribution to strengthening the supply chain and with the continuing challenges and delays from CMAM in executing the funds of the Global Fund Round 8 Phase 2 health systems strengthening grant, PMI will increase its share of technical assistance to CMAM in order to continue to support improvements in key areas such as warehousing, supervision, and logistics management information systems. PMI will also provide technical assistance to CMAM to improve its capacity to better liaise and strengthen communication and information exchange with the NMCP, continue to fortify human resources within CMAM, and improve warehousing management and logistics capabilities. PMI will continue to support the expansion of the SIMAM LMIS and will continue to support the ACT/RDT kitting system. Additionally, the EUV tool (see *Monitoring & Evaluation* section), together with the placement of the regional and provincial-level technical advisors will help information collection, aggregation, and timely delivery to CMAM to better inform all warehousing and procurement activities.

It is expected that the support from USG will be complemented by the Global Fund NFM health system strengthening component. This grant includes provision of technical assistance to CMAM to increase its capacity for generating, tracking, and monitoring of warehousing documentation. This will improve data collection for the LMIS and will help mitigate the potential for leakage of commodities. Additionally, CMAM's ability to conduct monthly periodic stock reconciliation and other routine quality assurance/quality control activities for basic warehouse management practices will be strengthened via technical assistance.

Proposed activities with FY 2016 funding: ($900,000)

- Supply chain strengthening: Support capacity building of CMAM to better plan for, deliver, and track malaria commodities. ($900,000)

5. Health system strengthening and capacity building

NMCP/PMI objectives
PMI supports a broad array of health system strengthening activities which cut across intervention areas, such as training of health workers, supply chain management, health information systems strengthening, drug quality monitoring, and NMCP capacity building.

One of the objectives of the 2012-2016 Malaria Strategic Plan is to ensure that all districts of the country have capacity to adequately manage and implement malaria control activities. Six main strategies were defined to achieve this goal: 1) review the organizational structure of the NMCP and equip it with appropriate human resources; 2) strengthen the infrastructure capacity and ensure adequate equipment for malaria control activities; 3) improve management and leadership at all levels of the program; 4) improve collaboration and coordination among partners; 5) improve malaria epidemic preparedness and response; and, 6) strengthen cross-border collaboration activities in order to support malaria elimination efforts in the Southern African Development Community region.

In keeping with the goals set forth in the Malaria Strategic Plan, PMI aims to:

1. Support human resources capacity through both pre- and in-service training and through supportive supervision in areas such as case management, malaria in pregnancy and BCC;
2. Support the design and implementation of key policy documents related to malaria control, including the development of the new National Strategic Plan, the revision of the Vector Control Strategy and the planning of community-based activities, particularly the expansion of the APE program; and
3. Support the strengthening of the management of medicines and medical supplies in order to ensure that the malaria-related commodities are available where needed.

Progress since PMI was launched
PMI is building capacity for malaria control at a number of levels. PMI resident advisors and implementing partners have provided technical and implementation support to the NMCP on a range of issues including development of strategic and operational plans, preparation of Global Fund applications and other key policy documents. PMI is also providing considerable support to strengthen the supply chain system (see *Pharmaceutical Management* section).

PMI supported the development of the Malaria Acceleration Plan, the Global Fund Round 9 Phase 2 proposal and the Global Fund NFM concept note. The Malaria Acceleration Plan is a multi-year operational plan of the malaria control strategy, covering the period of 2014 to 2016, which gives guidance on the timing for implementation for specific activities, on the parties responsible for implementation, and on funding availability.

PMI supported an entomologist at the NMCP to coordinate all vector control activities outside of Zambézia Province (where PMI provides direct support for IRS activities). In Zambézia Province, PMI has been strengthening the capacity of the DPS to implement IRS activities and conduct entomologic monitoring through the establishment of a regional entomology laboratory and insectary, which is staffed by DPS personnel who work with PMI's partner on these activities. The regional entomology capacity to do entomologic monitoring/surveillance has also been supported by PMI through the establishment of an entomology lab in Pemba, Cabo Delgado. In addition, PMI supported the refurbishment and equipment of the National Reference Laboratory, the entomology laboratory, and an insectary at INS.

PMI has supported several training activities, including the FELTP program. PMI supported the participation of two NMCP staff at an M&E training designed to provide participants with knowledge of M&E fundamentals and hands-on experience in designing M&E plans as they specifically relate to malaria programs. PMI also supported training in entomology with the objective of increasing capacity of INS and NMCP staff members to perform the CDC bottle assay technique, to detect mechanisms of insecticide resistance and to analyze, interpret and use entomological data. Three regional "training-of-trainers" for malaria microscopy were held in calendar year 2011 to establish a cadre of highly qualified master trainers. These trainings were led by CDC reference laboratorians and were very successful. Several technicians were chosen from among these master trainers to lead the national refresher training on malaria microscopic diagnosis. Moreover, PMI supported a needs assessment for the establishment of a quality control system for diagnostics in Mozambique; a draft guideline for such a system is awaiting approval. To complement this, two of the technicians working in the National Reference Laboratory traveled to Atlanta for a six-week training in molecular biology and other techniques that are seen as key activities of a diagnostic reference laboratory.

Given the lack of professionally trained health workers, the USG is contributing, along with other partners, to the revitalization of the APE system. The new APE system consists of community health workers who have been selected by their communities to undergo intensive four-month training on the prevention and treatment of common diseases, including malaria. Support for the APE revitalization comes from many partners, including UNICEF, USAID, World Bank, Irish Embassy, Malaria Consortium, Save the Children, and World Vision. The rollout of the APE trainings was divided into several rounds. Since the process began in calendar year 2011, 3,056 new APEs have been trained, and 3,041 of them are working.

Progress during the last 12-18 months
During the past fiscal year, PMI continued to support health system strengthening activities in order to increase Ministry of Health capacity to implement malaria related programs. Most of these activities were related to the strengthening of the logistic and supply chain systems for malaria commodities (see *Pharmaceutical Management* section for more details). The other important area of support was related to pre- and in-service training and supervision. PMI contributed to improve the capacity of NMCP staff in case management and malaria in pregnancy (see respective sections). PMI also continued to support the FELTP and supported the training of 128 community members in malaria BCC. These individuals were members of community health councils with responsibility for coordinating health activities in their community. They also act as community volunteers and facilitate BCC activities through group discussions or door-to-door visits.

PMI supported the Ministry of Health in addressing questions and comments related to the Global Fund NFM application. PMI also continued to support the Ministry of Health at central level to strengthen its APE program and the Global Fund unit. The MoH with support of USAID (using MCH funds), other donors, and other partners continued the expansion of the APE program, and 312 new APEs were trained nationwide, bringing the total to 3,056.

Recognizing the challenges faced by the MoH in the distribution of ITNs, PMI is working closely with NMCP and other partners to determine the best way forward. PMI is examining how distribution is conducted today, and how it could potentially change based on overall costs, benefits and risks. As a result of this exercise, PMI will produce several scenarios for ITN distribution that will be discussed with the MoH and other partners for consideration.

Finally, PMI continued to develop NMCP capacity to implement entomological monitoring activities nationwide (see IRS section for more details).

Field Epidemiology & Laboratory Training Program (FELTP):
PMI has provided technical assistance to two FELTP-led studies. The first is an evaluation of the MoH's mass distribution campaigns for ITNs, the first year of which took place in the fall of 2013; the second year of data collection occurred the fall of 2014. The study mirrors a similar one done in Sofala in calendar year 2010, and the data provided critical information about the performance of mass distribution campaigns in Nampula, as well as the impact on parasitemia among people who consistently used nets. The FELTP student presented the results of this study during a joint-FELTP/PMI presentation in March 2015. The second study PMI supported through FELTP is an investigation of a suspected nationwide increase in malaria cases. This study initially included a review of epidemiological trends of the past three years using routine data, followed by the drafting of a protocol to initially use routine data to investigate the suspected increase in cases, followed by on-site investigation using health facility and community data. The first phase of the investigation has been completed, and the second phase (field collection of data) is expected to begin in June 2015.

Plans and justification
Despite much progress on coverage and performance of malaria control activities, it is clear that more support is needed to improve service delivery quality and reliability. This is particularly true in the north of the country, where the burden is highest and a significant proportion of the population lives in rural settings. PMI will work to support the capacity of the Ministry of Health's provincial and district malaria focal points in Tete, Zambézia, Nampula and Cabo Delgado to better plan, manage, and analyze their activities with a goal of improving service quality at health facilities and at the community level. The malaria focal points are positions that already exist within the government structures, although many are currently being recruited. Their role is to coordinate malaria activities carried out by the MoH and its partners at a provincial and district level. PMI's resources will not support MoH salaries or positions, but will imbed technical assistance in the four provinces to build MoH capacity to improve service delivery and quality. Specific activities will be decided based on the situation in each province, although will largely focus on using available programmatic data to address supply, service provision and quality around case management and ANC services.

Previously identified weaknesses in case management and ANC service provision will be addressed through more directive and informed supervision from the provincial and district levels. PMI will work to leverage improvements in data collection and usage by district staff to schedule and guide supervision efforts. Where necessary, consumption data will be employed to ensure sufficient stocking levels and ensure facilities are ordering in a timely fashion from the *Via Classica.* This support will aim to ensure the linkages between the facility and district are strengthened and to capacitate the MoH malaria focal points to use data to guide their decision-making. The exact nature of the support will depend on the roll out of the DHIS-2 system in these provinces, but will work to ensure this system is in place and in use as soon as possible. This support must reach facilities in rural areas, where malaria burden is highest.

Other activities will focus on support to the Peace Corps, who have seen success on a range of prevention activities through their Stomp Out Malaria initiative. Support will also be provided for two FELTP positions to support post ITN campaign surveys, among other projects. PMI will also continue to support the capacity building efforts to the MoH's Global Fund Management Unit and central level support to the APE network. The support to the Global Fund unit will provide technical assistance to develop MoH capacity to design and execute Global Fund grants and improve coordination between the different MoH departments in the implementation of those grants. Similarly, the central support to the APE network will provide technical assistance to National APE program to improve coordination in MoH and with its partners.

Proposed activities with FY 2016 funding: ($1,423,500)

- Provincial level capacity building: Provide technical support to the MoH provincial and district level malaria focal points in PMI's four target provinces (10-20 districts each). These funds will not cover staff positions in the MoH, but will provided embedded technical assistance to build provincial and district level capacity to plan, manage and evaluate malaria activities. ($1,000,000)

- Peace Corps: Support two third year PCVs to assist in the implementation of community level activities around malaria prevention to be funded through SPA grants ($20,000 for two PCVs, $10,000 for SPA grants). ($30,000)

- FELTP: Support two FELTP fellows to design and implement the post ITN campaign survey, including field costs. ($150,000)

- Support central level planning: Continued technical assistance to the central MoH APE coordination department. ($100,000)

- Support GFATM Management Unit: Continued support to the MoH GFATM unit to improve coordination and planning of grant development and implementation. ($143,500)

Table VIII: Health Systems Strengthening Activities

HSS Building Block	Technical Area	Description of Activity
Health Services	Case Management & MIP	Supporting more intensive and data driven facility level supervision of health worker performance for fever case management and MIP services.
Health Workforce	Malaria diagnosis	Building provincial level capacity to manage case management supervision activities and implement cascade trainings to health facilities.
Health Information	Monitoring & Evaluation	Supporting the roll out of DHIS-2 and investing in support of provincial and district level malaria focal points to collect and use data to drive programmatic decision-making.
	Entomological Monitoring	Scaling up entomological monitoring and building the NMCP capacity to carry out these activities to identify and characterize vector populations and insecticide resistance.
Essential Medical Products, Vaccines, and Technologies	Case Management	Supporting CMAM to more effectively plan and manage malaria commodities by ordering from districts and facilities through the *Via Classica*.
Health Finance	GF Management Support	Continuing capacity building of the MoH's Global Fund management unit to ensure timely and accurate submissions and, thus, efficient use of Global Fund funds.
Leadership and Governance	BCC	Supporting the Malaria Communications Working Group to develop a national BCC strategy and related materials.
	Vector Control	Supporting the development of the updated integrated vector control strategy to account for the emergence of pyrethroid resistance and universal ITN distribution.

6. Behavior change communication

NMCP/PMI objectives

The objective of the NMCP's BCC activities is to ensure that by calendar year 2016, 100% of the population is covered by key messages related to malaria prevention, diagnosis, and treatment. PMI supports a range of BCC activities aimed at promoting correct and consistent use of ITNs, increasing acceptance of IRS, and increasing adherence to treatment and prevention therapies; all of which are key to achieving and maintaining the NMCP's goals for malaria prevention and control. To coordinate all malaria communications activities, the MoH has created a malaria communication group. This group includes representatives from the NMCP, the

Communications Department of the MoH, donors, United Nations agencies, and implementing partners. This working group is chaired by the NMCP and is supposed to meet once a month.

In alignment with the GRM, PMI aims to achieve the following objectives:
1. Strengthen the capacity of MoH/DEPROS to effectively develop, implement, and coordinate malaria BCC strategies and approaches.
2. Build the capacity of local organizations to train religious leaders in BCC and community mobilization to reduce malaria prevalence.
3. Develop in-country capacity, within the NMCP and PMI implementing partners, to effectively monitor and evaluate the quality of BCC activities and their impact on desired behavioral outcomes.

Progress since PMI was launched
Since 2007, PMI has continued to support malaria BCC through a variety of channels, including a consortium of religious groups that provides malaria messages to communities during religious sermons as well as door-to-door malaria BCC activities outside of the religious sphere through community volunteers. PMI has also provided central level capacity building support for BCC to the NMCP and, more recently, DEPROS to develop the overall malaria communication strategy as well as implement and coordinate malaria BCC activities in Mozambique. However, there remains limited technical capacity for BCC at the NMCP, and the coordination between the malaria program and DEPROS is weak. PMI is the main donor supporting malaria BCC activities in Mozambique. Global Fund provides limited support to community-based BCC activities in the context of large-scale universal coverage campaigns of ITNs. Although there has been progress in some areas, including the development of a national malaria BCC strategy in calendar year 2013, BCC related to malaria prevention and control continues to be a notable weakness in Mozambique.

Progress during the last 12-18 months
During the past year, PMI continued its support to BCC activities, both at the policy and operational levels. At the policy level, PMI continued to support the operationalization of the NMCP communication and advocacy strategy. A desk review was carried out to gather and analyze regional and country data regarding perceptions, acceptability and use of malaria prevention, diagnosis and treatment interventions, from both health care provider and client perspectives. As a result of this review, two priorities were identified: 1) the need for more coordination and visibility of malaria BCC interventions, and 2) the need for technical strengthening of the NMCP communication division and of DEPROS. PMI also continued to provide technical assistance to the Malaria Communications Working Group, by providing strategic guidance to strengthen the coordination capacity of the NMCP and DEPROS and by supporting regular meetings. With PMI support, the NMCP finalized its branding strategy, which consists of a slogan, "Malaria Out! Protected and Strong Families", with a logo representing a family.

At the operational level, PMI continued to support the dissemination of malaria messages through integrated provincial-level platforms in Nampula and Zambézia. These platforms, which receive funding from multiple health elements, are able to maximize resources and ensure BCC is comprehensively addressed. These platforms have a significant reach within PMI's targeted provinces and utilize various proven BCC channels, including door-to-door mobilization, community radio, theater groups, and training of health workers, among other channels to influence malaria-related behaviors at the community and health facility level using approved messages. Over the past 12 months, 93 new Committee Health Councils (CHCs) were created and 163 group education sessions were carried out at the community-level, reaching a total of 356,367 people, of whom 57% were women. Several media activities were also implemented, including the development and dissemination of 2,548 radio spots. The radio spots were aired three times per week in Portuguese and in the local language of each province. A total of six episodes of TV programs were broadcasted on the main television stations addressing issues related to bed net promotion and IPTp.

To strengthen its community-based BCC activities, PMI launched an integrated malaria and diarrhea prevention campaign in Nicoadala, in partnership with local authorities and other partners. The major objective of the campaign was to create awareness and provide an opportunity for the community to participate in the design and implementation of malaria interventions. The campaign involved several activities including a public march headed by the Nicoadala District Administrator, health fairs, distribution of bed nets, road-shows, radio programs and spots, door-to-door outreach, practical demonstrations of the correct use of bed nets, and video sessions followed by community dialogues. The messages focused mainly on promotion and use of bed nets, IPTp and the need to promptly seek health care in cases of suspected malaria.

During the past fiscal year, PMI continued to support faith based BCC channels, which worked in targeted districts in Zambézia, Nampula, Sofala, Inhambane, and Gaza Provinces. This support continued to provide inter-personal messaging related to malaria prevention and treatment in which 25,150 people were reached, while also reaching another 12,751 people during door-to-door visits. These visits offer the opportunity to strengthen the capacity of families to prevent malaria, by teaching basic skills such as how to hang a bed net.

PMI also implemented community mobilization activities in Zambézia Province to increase acceptance of the PMI-supported IRS program, which took place in four districts. The community sensitization activities were based on messages approved by the NMCP and included the involvement of local leaders in all steps of the campaign and the training of these leaders to mobilize their communities. In coordination with the NMCP, a television spot to support the national IRS campaign was also produced and aired.

Lastly, PMI continued to support one third-year Malaria Peace Corps volunteer (PCV) in Maputo to coordinate malaria-related activities by the nearly 200 PCVs nationwide. All PCVs were trained on malaria three times within their period of service and have been catalysts for the uptake of positive malaria prevention and treatment behaviors within their communities. PMI-funded small project assistance grants have allowed PCVs to promote malaria messages through trainings and workshops, music videos, murals and blogs. Finally, PMI, through Peace Corps, formed a partnership with a local mobile phone company, Vodacom. Vodacom is providing bed nets to be distributed by PCVs in the villages they work and also provides a platform for dissemination of malaria messages through mobile phones.

Plans and justification
In FY 2016 PMI will work to further build the capacity of the Malaria Communications Working Group to consolidate BCC materials and approaches, while also continuing to scale up

community level activities to deliver these messages. The successfully implemented World Malaria Day activities using the newly developed malaria branding provided a platform on which to build further activities and approaches. PMI will provide support centrally to coordinate these activities and develop a robust and comprehensive malaria BCC package for use throughout the country.

The BCC package will be available to all malaria partners in the country to use and will contain standardized messages that link to the national malaria "brand" developed for World Malaria Day. Messages will be developed for all key interventions and will encourage uptake and use of ITNs, attendance are ANC for pregnant women, timely treatment seeking behavior and the risks of presumptive treatment of fever. The aim of these efforts will be to empower targeted populations to seek and demand effective services to prevent and treat malaria effectively. This package will take advantage of all feasible channels and ensure that health care providers are also employed to act as channels for malaria messages.

These materials will be available for all to use throughout the country; however, PMI will focus its BCC implementation in the four key provinces of Tete, Zambezia, Nampula, and Cabo Delgado through a mix of community level interpersonal communication (IPC), health care provider training and suitable mass media activities to reach, particularly, those in rural communities with high quality standardized messages to promote behaviors such as ITN usage, ANC attendance and prompt treatment seeking behavior.

Proposed activities with FY 2016 funding: ($1,217,500)

- Central level coordination of BCC activities: Support to the Malaria Communications Working Group to develop standardized malaria BCC materials for use throughout Mozambique. ($200,000)

- Provincial coordination and roll out of BCC activities: Working with provincial and district malaria focal points, in addition to local community groups to plan and implement BCC campaigns in high burden provinces. ($800,000)

- Support faith based community BCC activities: Working with faith-based organizations to target standardized malaria messages through faith based channels and community led activities. ($217,500)

7. Monitoring and evaluation

NMCP/PMI objectives
The M&E plan 2012–2016 is a tool for monitoring and evaluating the Malaria Strategic Plan 2012–2016 (MSP). The M&E plan was developed in a participatory way by the NMCP M&E technical working group, partners, and stakeholders.

The objectives of the M&E plan are[3]:

a) Guide the periodic tracking and documentation of the implementation of the Malaria Strategic Plan so as to ensure accountability and address problems that emerge in a timely manner.
b) Guide collection, processing, and use of malaria data for decision-making at all levels.
c) Provide a framework for measuring the outcomes and impact of scale-up of interventions against targets.
d) Provide a framework for providing feedback to data providers and disseminating malaria information to all stakeholders.
e) Provide an action plan for strengthening malaria M&E capacity.

Sources of data and information will include the routine health information system, integrated disease surveillance system, activity reports from the districts and implementing partners, periodic household and facility surveys as well as operational research studies.

PMI's support to M&E in Mozambique aligns with the NMCP's M&E plan. PMI coordinates and collaborates with the NMCP and several partners in providing technical assistance and resources for M&E activities, including MIP activities. PMI participates in the NMCP M&E technical working group that is comprised of several NMCP staff and other MoH departments (Health Information Department, M&E department, and the Public Health Directorate M&E unit) as well as the NMCP's partners. The NMCP M&E unit leads the coordination of this technical working group, which meets monthly and more regularly when issues arise. National surveys are implemented in coordination with the National Statistics Institute (also referred to as INE for Instituto Nacional de Estatísticas) and the National Health Institute (also referred to as INS for Instituto Nacional de Saúde).

Hierarchy of M&E in the MoH:

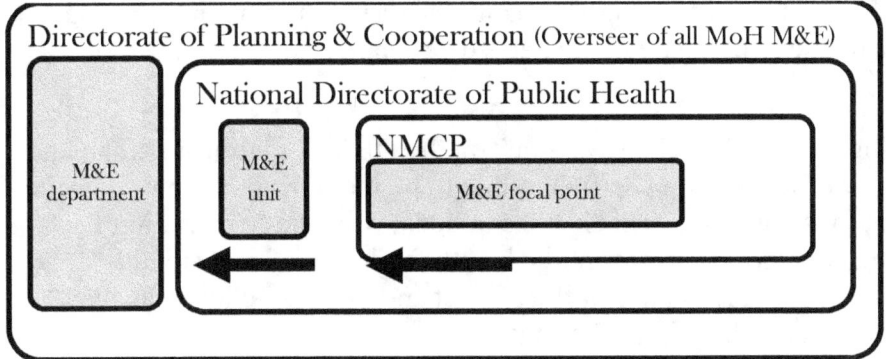

---

[3] *NMCP Monitoring and Evaluation Plan 2012–2016*

Routine Health Information System

The Health Management Information System (HMIS, or SIS *for Sistema de Informação para Saúde*) is an electronic system called the *Modulo Basico*. All basic in- and out-patient data from health facilities is reported through the *Modulo Basico* system. The key indicators that will rely on HMIS as a data source are:

- Total in-patient malaria deaths
- In-patient malaria cases
- Total outpatient malaria cases (confirmed and clinical)
- Malaria positivity rate
- Proportion of suspected cases tested for malaria

HMIS data are collected on paper-based tools at health facilities and sent monthly to the district level where they are collated, entered into an electronic database, and then transferred through USB flash drives to the province information unit. The aggregated data is emailed to the central level Health Information Department in the Directorate of Planning and Cooperation. To date, this system has not provided sufficient quality data for the NMCP and is in the process of being replaced by a DHIS-2-based system called *Sistema de Informação para a Saúde – Monitoria e Avaliação* (SIS-MA). An interim malaria database that was created to collect data from outpatient registers, pharmacies, and laboratories is being used until the SIS-MA can be fully rolled out. The interim system extracts malaria-specific data from existing registers using parallel malaria data reporting forms. These forms are sent to malaria focal points at the district level. The district focal point then compiles the data and sends them to the provincial level where data from all districts will be entered into a malaria database.

PMI has been supporting malaria surveillance in eight districts in Zambézia Province (present or previous IRS districts) for the last few years. A surveillance coordinator assisted with training health providers on the new malaria tools and in 2014 collected copies of the weekly *Boletim Epidemiologico Semanal* (BES) from 24 targeted health facilities during monthly monitoring visits. The coordinator was then able to compare the malaria data reported through the two surveillance systems.

In 2014, PMI supported training of three NMCP M&E staff on the DHIS-2 platform. At the end of the training, the staff had created a malaria-specific module to be included in the new system by digitizing the existing data reporting forms. This has the added advantage of obviating the need for additional training on data reporting forms at the health facility level and should minimize the amount of additional training needed at the district and provincial level, as they should be effectively the same forms with a digital interface.

Integrated disease surveillance system

All public health facilities are expected to report the number of confirmed malaria cases on a weekly basis through the bulletin for notifiable diseases, BES is a sub-system of the HMIS and is managed by the Department of Epidemiology. Malaria is one of ten notifiable diseases. However, confirmed and clinical cases are not reported separately on a routine basis, limiting the quality of the data. Inpatient and outpatient registers from health facilities are the data source for both the BES and HMIS. In 2011 a process to revise the BES standard operating procedures manual began and the NMCP, as part of the technical working group, collaborated with the epidemiology department to revise the BES tools to allow for the distinction between confirmed and clinical cases.

Surveys
National Level Surveys- PMI supported a Demographic and Health Survey that was undertaken in 2011. PMI has supported ITN universal coverage surveys. The planned AIS/MIS was postponed until June 2015. The first MIS was in 2007 and a Multiple Indicator Cluster Survey (MICS) occurred in 2008.

End-Use Verification (EUV) Surveys- PMI-supported EUVs have been taking place since 2011. Province and site selection is done in collaboration with the NMCP. Within each district, one urban health unit (health center or hospital), one rural health center, and one APE are also included. In addition, at the request of the NMCP, these surveys have been broadened to include a range of malaria activities. This includes laboratory, pharmacy, and case management components, where samples of medical records from previous months are pulled and data is extracted to calculate various indicators on case management.

Therapeutic efficacy monitoring
See Case Management Section

Capacity Building
In 2011, Malaria Control and Evaluation Partnerships in Africa placed an M&E advisor in Mozambique to assist the NMCP and partners to better coordinate M&E activities. The M&E advisor played a central role in guiding the process of finalizing the M&E strategic document, as well as the National Malaria Policy and National Strategic Plan; however, this position no longer exists. The ongoing M&E coordination among stakeholders is critically important for the NMCP to have appropriate information to manage the program. PMI identified an M&E advisor that was placed at the NMCP with funds from the Office of the Global AIDS Coordinator. PMI has also supported the participation of NMCP staff at a malaria M&E training in Ghana.

Entomological Monitoring
See IRS section

Data flow within Mozambique

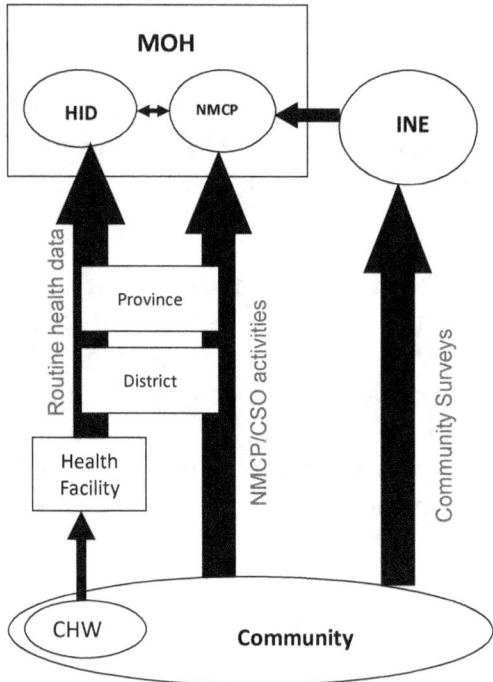

The data flow diagram comes from the NMCP Monitoring and Evaluation Plan 2012–2016. The NMCP/CSO activities would include any monitoring and evaluations carried out by those institutions (laboratory department data, ITN and IRS data). Community surveys would not be national surveys, but could be a local household survey carried out by the INE or others. Unfortunately, there is no feedback loop at this time, but PMI is working on that weakness.

Progress during the last 12-18 months

Routine Health Information System
The interim system was to be a temporary system that could provide data until a more permanent, DHIS-2-based system could be implemented. Trainings for the new outpatient registers have taken place in all 11 provinces, although the inconsistency in translating the provincial level trainings to districts and health facilities has resulted in incomplete use of the system. Currently only three provinces use and submit the new forms on a monthly basis.

Because of delays in identifying a mechanism and partner to implement and rollout DHIS-2, PMI has not provided any financial support to the system in the past 12 months. Instead, support has centered on improving the use and quality of the data reported through BES and the new forms. This support has included using routine data to produce the annual report that included descriptions of epidemiological trends over the past three years, evaluation of a suspected national increase in cases using routine data sources, and generation of a malaria-specific database to house all relevant routine malaria data reported through all systems.

PMI has supported data audits, data quality improvement, and data use in four districts in the Sofala Province and three districts in the Manica Province. In Zambézia Province, PMI supported supervision and capacity building at health facilities to improve the data collection and reporting practices from the facility to the central level in eight districts. Reporting completeness in these districts was found to be 94%. The testing rate across the health facilities was 99%.

The DHIS-2 is being rolled out in Maputo Province through *Centro de Investigacao em Saúde da Manhica* (CISM). CISM was able to speed up the process by providing provincial-wide training followed by implementation in specific districts in Maputo Province. Global Fund and PEPFAR have been funding the development and rollout for DHIS-2 at the provincial level. Global Fund has ring-fenced $3.5 million for the DHIS-2 rollout. As a result, it is likely that the system will be rolled out in PMI's target provinces in 6-9 months. PMI will then support the roll out of the system at the district level in its priority provinces.

Surveys

National level survey: PMI has contributed funds towards the implementation of the AIS/MIS, which will collect nationally representative data on malaria prevalence and prevention measures, including ITN coverage and use. This study was originally scheduled to begin in July 2014, but due to delays associated with presidential elections, has been postponed. The new start date is set for June 2015.

End-use Verification Surveys: The EUV tool has been implemented quarterly in Mozambique over the past 12 months. The last report from the EUV is for April 2015. Eighteen percent of health facilities sampled were stocked out of all ACTs and consequently would not be able to treat malaria cases. The facilities had varying degrees (29%–76%) of stock outs of the ACT presentations. The EUV also reported an 18% stock out of RDTs. Case management indicators showed malaria accounting for 15% of cases seen, with 96% receiving a test (75% RDT and 21% microcopy). Children under the age of five years accounted for 67% of cases and all were treated with an ACT.

Mid-Term Review

The Mozambique Mid-Term Review (MTR) of the 2012-2016 National Malaria Prevention and Control Strategic Plan was completed in July 2014. The MTR was conducted under the leadership and coordination of the MoH/NMCP with support from malaria control partners and stakeholders. The MTR assessed the progress made against the goals, objectives, and targets outlined in the plan, identified the key challenges hindering progress, and recommend improvements for performance to assure impact in the remaining period of the National Malaria Strategic Plan 2012-2016.

The MTR had four major conclusions:

1. Great strides have been made on malaria control, and if efforts are continued, the country will succeed in achieving control.
2. There has been remarkable achievement on the impact and outcome indicators.
3. The current program goals are attainable given the current level of performance.
4. Although great impact has been made on morbidity and mortality, more could have been achieved with greater decentralization.

In turn, recommendations focused on increased decentralization of control activities, intensification of cross-border activities, increasing accountability at all levels, greater emphasis on monitoring of program implementation, improvement of data quality and completeness, and increasing the domestic budget.

Impact Evaluation

An Impact Evaluation was undertaken in Mozambique during 2014 and the report released in August 2015. According to the draft report, progress was seen with nearly all indicators: net ownership among children under 5 years of age increased from 37% to 57% between 2007 and 2011, whereas use increased from 7% to 36% during the same time period. The percentage of women who received at least 2 doses of SP increased from 16% in 2007 to 19% in 2011, while the percentage of children under 5 with fever during the previous weeks that were treated with an antimalarial increased from 15% in 2007 to 30% in 2011. Overall, parasitemia in children 6-59 months of age decreased from 52% in 2007 to 36% in 2011, while all-cause mortality in children under 5 years of age decreased from 152 to 97 during the same time period.

Table IX. Monitoring and Evaluation Data Sources

Data Source	Survey Activities	2010	2011	2012	2013	2014	2015	2016	2017
National-level Household surveys	Demographic Health Survey (DHS)		x						
	Malaria Indicator Survey (MIS)						X		
	AIS								
Health Facility and Other Surveys	Health facility survey						X		
	SPA survey								
	EUV survey		x	x	x	x	x	x	x
	Support to HMIS	x	x	x	x	x	x	x	x
Therapeutic Efficacy Monitoring	In vivo efficacy testing	x	x				x		x
Entomology	Entomological surveillance and resistance monitoring	x	x	x	x	x	x	x	x
Other Data Sources	Malaria Impact Evaluation					X			

Plans and justification

In alignment with the GRM, PMI aims to achieve the following objectives: 1) Provide support for provincial and district-level supervision and training of health workers and district and provincial M&E personnel on the collection and reporting of routine malaria data; 2) Support malaria data analysis and use at district, provincial, and central level to enable data-driven decision making; and 3) Support the transition from *Módulo Básico* to SIS-MA (DHIS-2) in four targeted provinces.

As the country transitions to the DHIS-2 platform, the BES will not be needed at a national level. However, PMI has been meeting with CHAI, CISM, the NMCP, and the Department of Epidemiology to consider continuing the BES as an epidemic detection system for the pre-elimination areas of the south that require reporting more frequently than the monthly SIS-MA.

PMI is also supporting durability monitoring of bed nets and post-campaign evaluations in three provinces. The monitoring protocol has been finalized and submitted for ethical clearance. Data collection is planned to start during the third quarter of 2015 and continue for three years.

Proposed activities with FY 2016 funding: ($1,270,000)

- Provincial level M&E support: Support provincial and district level trainings during roll out of DHIS-2 in four targeted provinces. Strengthen surveillance and M&E at the health facility, district, and provincial levels in four targeted provinces (Nampula, Zambézia, Cabo Delgado, and Tete), to ensure proper data collection and reporting practices, as well as malaria data analysis and use for planning and decision making. Some districts will need to focus initially on improving the quality and completeness of facility data; others can begin analyzing and using existing data while continuing to work on quality, completeness, and timeliness. ($800,000)

- DHIS-2 roll-out: Supporting the national effort to maintain the country's DHIS-2 management information system. ($150,000)

- EUV Surveys: Support the implementation of the quarterly EUV surveys in a sample of health facilities and medical stores. ($100,000)

- CDC M&E Technical Assistance: In support of DHIS-2 and analysis, interpretation, and use of routine health data. ($20,000)

- Durability monitoring: Includes continued support for monitoring the physical durability and insecticide retention of ITNs distributed in 2015. ($200,000)

8. Operational research

NMCP/PMI objectives
Operational research (OR) has been identified as a priority for the MoH. Specific guidelines for OR are being developed at the national level, and general priority questions to be targeted for OR for each priority disease have been identified. The NMCP has the goal of first defining specific research priorities within each of its programmatic areas, and then secondly to define roles and responsibilities for the NMCP, INS, CISM, the OR center in Beira, and external partners, for each of these research areas.

In line with the MoH objectives, PMI aims to achieve the following objectives:

1. Support the development of an OR agenda for the NMCP.
2. Work with MoH to define roles and responsibilities for malaria research in Mozambique.

3. Support implementation of OR activities that focus on the NMCP's identified priority areas.

Progress since PMI was launched
The two primary local organizations conducting operational research on malaria in Mozambique are CISM and the INS. Historically, there have been challenges with communication and sharing of priorities between the organizations. Although there are still obstacles that need to be overcome, with the initiation of pre-elimination activities by CISM in Maputo Province, more opportunities for addressing key OR questions now exist in the country.

Progress during the last 12-18 months
A high-level MoH meeting was held in February 2014 to both build a list of key research questions that need to be addressed to help the NMCP better implement their activities, and to create a roadmap with established roles and responsibilities of key partners. To this end, a draft priority OR list has been generated, and plans are under way to hold a joint NMCP-INS workshop on OR for malaria.

Table X. PMI-funded Operational Research Studies

Planned OR Studies FY 2016			
Title	**Start date (est.)**	**End date (est.)**	**Budget**
Community Level Impact of Switching from Pyrethroid IRS to Organophosphate IRS	April 2016	April 2017	$120,000
Impact of District Level Changes to Vector Control Interventions	Sept 2016	April 2018	$300,000

Plans and justification
The anemia and parasitemia survey originally planned to begin with FY 2014 reprogrammed funds has been rethought based on the emergence of pyrethroid resistance data and instead now has been divided into two smaller studies described below to answer two distinct questions. The FY 2014 funds slated for an OR activity will instead be used to buy long-lasting organophosphate insecticide for the 2015 IRS campaign.

With reprogrammed FY 2015 funds, PMI will support community level parasitemia surveys to determine the impact of IRS in one district in Zambezia Province, including the switch from pyrethroid IRS in 2015 to organophosphate IRS in 2016. These surveys will be complemented by entomological data collection, as well as data collected at health facilities within the community catchment areas.

With FY 2016 funds, PMI plans to fund one OR activity. This activity is a two-year parasitemia study in two districts in Zambézia that will build off PMI's epidemiological surveillance activities at health facilities in current and former IRS districts, as well as ongoing entomological monitoring. The goal of this project is to couple health facility and entomological data with data on the community prevalence of disease to evaluate the impact of different combinations of vector control methods, in particular evaluating the addition of organophosphate IRS on top of ITNs and switching from blanket organophosphate IRS to universal ITN coverage. Community prevalence data will be collected before and after the transmission season. These data will be combined with entomological and disease incidence data collected in these districts to guide the NMCP in refining their vector control strategy. This activity is in line with the NMCP's identified priority OR area of collecting data to improve decision making ability on vector control. Moreover, discussions are underway for this work to be undertaken as part of an IRS cost-effectiveness trial under a UNITAID proposal that has been accepted for a market intervention to accelerate the uptake of long-lasting, non-pyrethroid IRS.

Proposed activities with FY 2016 funding: *($300,000)*

- Impact of District Level Changes to Vector Control Interventions: Community parasitemia surveys in Zambezia. ($300,000)

9. Staffing and administration

Two health professionals serve as resident advisors to oversee PMI in Mozambique, one representing CDC and one representing USAID. In addition, two Foreign Service Nationals work as part of the PMI team. All PMI staff members are part of a single interagency team led by the USAID Mission Director or his/her designee in country. The PMI team shares responsibility for development and implementation of PMI strategies and work plans, coordination with national authorities, managing collaborating agencies and supervising day-to-day activities. Candidates for resident advisor positions (whether initial hires or replacements) will be evaluated and/or interviewed jointly by USAID and CDC, and both agencies will be involved in hiring decisions, with the final decision made by the individual agency.

PMI professional staff work together to oversee all technical and administrative aspects of PMI, including finalizing details of the project design, implementing malaria prevention and treatment activities, M&E of outcomes and impact, reporting of results, and providing guidance to PMI partners.

The PMI lead in country is the USAID Mission Director. The day-to-day lead for PMI is delegated to the USAID Health Office Director and thus the two PMI resident advisors, one from USAID and one from CDC, report to the USAID Health Office Director for day-to-day leadership and work together as a part of a single interagency team. The technical expertise housed in Atlanta and Washington guides PMI programmatic efforts.

The two PMI resident advisors are based within the USAID health office and are expected to spend approximately half their time sitting with and providing technical assistance to the NMCP and partners.

Locally-hired staff to support PMI activities either in Ministries or in USAID will be approved by the USAID Mission Director. Because of the need to adhere to specific country policies and USAID accounting regulations, any transfer of PMI funds directly to ministries or host governments will need to be approved by the USAID Mission Director and Controller, in addition to the US Global Malaria Coordinator.

Proposed activities with FY 2016 funding: *($1,050,000)*

1. In-country PMI staff salaries, benefits, travel, and other PMI administrative costs: Continued support for two PMI (CDC and USAID) Resident Advisors and two Foreign Service nationals staff members to oversee activities supported by PMI in Mozambique. ($500,000 USAID; $550,000 CDC)

Table 1: Budget Breakdown by Mechanism

President's Malaria Initiative – Mozambique

Planned Malaria Obligations for FY 2016

Mechanism	Geographic Area	Activity	Budget ($)	%
TBD - Supply Chain Contract	Nationwide	Procure ITNs	3,720,000	48%
	Nationwide	Support ANC distribution of ITNs	1,900,000	
	Nationwide	Procure ACTs	4,950,000	
	Nationwide	Procure RDTs	2,700,000	
	Nationwide	Supply chain strengthening	900,000	
	Nationwide	End-use verification surveys	100,000	
IRS 2 TO6	Zambezia	IRS Implementation in Zambezia Province	6,000,000	24%
	Nationwide	Entomological monitoring	500,000	
	Nationwide	Support to national government IRS program	400,000	
GEMS II	Zambezia	IRS environmental assessment	30,000	<1%
CISM	Nationwide	Post-campaign survey	300,000	2%

Mechanism	Geographic Area	Activity	Budget ($)	%
	Zambezia	Impact of district level changes to vector control interventions	300,000	
JHU/VectorWorks	Nationwide	Campaign planning and distribution TA support	100,000	1%
	Nationwide	Durability monitoring	200,000	
TBD (Malaria bilateral)	Tete, Zambezia, Nampula, Cabo Delgado	ANC training and supervision	250,000	8%
		Provincial, district, and health center level support of case management and training	350,000	
		Provincial level capacity building	450,000	
		Provincial coordination and roll out of BCC activities	800,000	
		Provincial level M&E support	400,000	
		DHIS-2 roll out	150,000	
MCSP	Nationwide	Support national MIP planning and implementation	250,000	6%
	Tete, Zambézia, Nampula, Cabo Delgado ("lite" in Zambezia and Tete)	ANC training and supervision	250,000	
		Provincial, district, and health center level support of case management and training	350,000	
		Provincial level capacity building	500,000	
		Provincial level M&E support	400,000	
DANIDA	Tete	Provincial level capacity building	50,000	< 1%
MalariaCare	Tete, Cabo Delgado	Diagnosis and treatment support for training and supervision	500,000	2%
	Maputo	Central level laboratory support	250,000	

Mechanism	Geographic Area	Activity	Budget ($)	%
Peace Corps	Nationwide	Support to community BCC activities	30,000	<1%
TBD (BCC bilateral)	Nationwide	Central level coordination of BCC activities	200,000	1%
PIRCOM	Nationwide	Faith-based community BCC activities	217,500	1%
TBD (System strengthening bilateral)	Nationwide	Support central level planning	243,500	1%
CDC/IAA	Nationwide	Entomological technical assistance	29,000	3%
	Nationwide	Laboratory strengthening technical assistance	10,000	
	Nationwide	M&E technical assistance	20,000	
	Nationwide	FELTP support to post campaign survey	150,000	
	Nationwide	Staffing and administration	550,000	
USAID	Nationwide	Staffing and administration	500,000	2%
Total			**$ 29,000,000**	**100%**

Table 2: Budget Breakdown by Activity

President's Malaria Initiative – Mozambique

Planned Malaria Obligations for FY 2016

Proposed Activity	Mechanism	Budget		Geographic Area	Description
		Total $	Commodity $		
		PREVENTIVE ACTIVITIES			
Insecticide-treated Nets					
Procure ITNs	TBD - Supply Chain Contract	3,720,000	3,720,000	Nationwide	Procurement of approximately 1,130,700 ITNs for distribution through routine ANC services.
Support ANC distribution of ITNs	TBD - Supply Chain Contract	1,900,000		Nationwide	Distribution costs for approximately 1,130,700 ITNs from the port of entry to district level warehouses.
Post-campaign survey	CISM	300,000		Nationwide	Household survey to evaluate the coverage and usage of ITNs delivered through GFATM supported mass distribution campaigns.
Campaign planning and distribution TA support	VectorWorks	100,000		Nationwide	Due to the complexity and logistical challenge of mass distribution in Mozambique, technical assistance to the nation campaign will be needed to ensure efficient planning and implementation.
SUBTOTAL ITNs		6,020,000	3,720,000		
Indoor Residual Spraying					
IRS implementation in Zambezia Province	IRS 2 TO6	6,000,000		Zambezia	Implementation costs for IRS activities to cover approximately 4 districts. While currently planned for Zambezia, the updated national integrated vector control strategy may necessitate a shift in geographic focus. All insecticide (organophosphate) will be covered by Global Fund.

Proposed Activity	Mechanism	Budget		Geographic Area	Description
		Total $	Commodity $		
Entomological monitoring	IRS 2 TO6	500,000		Zambezia	Continuation of entomological monitoring and insecticide resistance monitoring. Currently planned for Zambezia though the updated national integrated vector control strategy may necessitate a shift in geographic focus.
Support to national government IRS program	IRS 2 TO6	400,000		Nationwide	Support for training of trainers to supervise MoH IRS implementation and environmental compliance activities, particularly in light of new insecticides being introduced to the GRM program.
IRS environmental assessment	GEMS II	30,000		Zambezia	Routine environmental assessment to monitor IRS activities; recommended every 2 years
Entomological TA	CDC/IAA	29,000		Nationwide	Two TDY visits from CDC entomology branch to build MoH entomological monitoring capacity.
SUBTOTAL IRS		**6,959,000**	**0**		
Malaria in Pregnancy					
Support national MIP planning and implementation	MCSP	250,000		Nationwide	Support to the central level planning and coordination of MIP activities, particularly its continuing integration into standard ANC packages. Will include planning the rollout of updated IPTp guidelines.
ANC training and supervision	MCSP (in Zambezia and Tete)	250,000		Tete, Zambezia, Nampula, Cabo Delgado	Concerted provincial, district and facility level support for the improvement of service delivery of key MIP interventions. To be coordinated with other provincially focused activities to improve supervision, monitoring and performance improvement of MIP services in four target provinces.
	TBD (Malaria bilateral)	250,000			
SUBTOTAL MIP		**750,000**			
SUBTOTAL PREVENTIVE		**13,729,000**			

CASE MANAGEMENT

65

Diagnosis and Treatment

Proposed Activity	Mechanism	Budget		Geographic Area	Description
		Total $	Commodity $		
Procure ACTs	TBD - Supply Chain Contract	4,950,000	4,950,000	Nationwide	Procurement of 5 million treatments of the national first-line antimalarial (artemether-lumefantrine). Commodities to be pooled and distributed nationally.
Procure RDTs	TBD - Supply Chain Contract	2,700,000	2,700,000	Nationwide	Procurement of 9 million single-species RDTs. Commodities to be pooled and distributed nationally.
Provincial, district, and health center level support of case management and training	MCSP (in Zambezia and Tete)	350,000		Tete, Zambezia, Nampula, Cabo Delgado	Concerted provincial, district and facility level support for the improvement of service delivery of key febrile case management interventions. To be coordinated with other provincially focused activities to improve supervision, monitoring and performance improvement of case management services in four target provinces.
	TBD (Malaria bilateral)	350,000			
Central level laboratory support	MalariaCare	250,000		Maputo	Support to build national level laboratory capacity and improve the quality and performance of national referral facilities.
Diagnosis and treatment support for training and supervision	MalariaCare	500,000		Tete and Cabo Delgado	Capacity building support to roll out best practices in the training and supervision of malaria diagnosis in two target provinces.
Laboratory strengthening TA	CDC/IAA	10,000		Nationwide	A TDY from CDC Atlanta to support national laboratory diagnosis capacity building.

Pharmaceutical Management

Proposed Activity	Mechanism	Total $	Commodity $	Geographic Area	Description
Supply chain strengthening support	TBD - Supply Chain Contract	900,000		Nationwide	Working with CMAM to improve logistical planning and implementation through better use of data and building skills of key personnel at both the national and provincial levels
SUBTOTAL CASE MANAGEMENT		**10,010,000**	**7,650,000**		

HEALTH SYSTEM STRENGTHENING / CAPACITY BUILDING

Proposed Activity	Mechanism	Total $	Commodity $	Geographic Area	Description
Provincial level capacity building	MCSP (in Zambezia and Tete)	500,000		Tete, Zambezia, Nampula, Cabo Delgado	Support in four target provinces to improve the planning and coordination of malaria control activities. The support will focus on data collection, assessment and use in strategic decision making as well as capacity building for provincial and

Proposed Activity	Mechanism	Budget		Geographic Area	Description
		Total $	Commodity $		
	TBD (Malaria bilateral)	450,000			district level MoH managers.
	DANIDA	50,000			
Support to community BCC activities	Peace Corps	30,000		Nationwide	Support for two third-year Peace Corps volunteers to coordinate PCV malaria prevention activities at community level. Includes funding for SPA grants to support these activities.
FELTP support to post campaign survey	CDC/IAA	150,000		Nampula	Dedicated FELTP support to research objectives, with particular focus on the post campaign survey and, possibly, IRS OR activities.
Support central level planning	TBD (System Strengthening bilateral)	243,500		Maputo	Continuing the crucial support to the central level planning department for the APE network in addition to ongoing assistance and capacity building to the MoH's GFATM management unit.
SUBTOTAL HSS & CAPACITY BUILDING		**1,423,500**			
BEHAVIOR CHANGE COMMUNICATION					
Central level coordination of BCC activities	TBD (BCC bilateral)	200,000		Maputo	Support to the NMCP Communications Working Group to develop core BCC materials and build on the national malaria branding developed for the 2015 World Malaria Day. This activity will develop a national level package for use my all malaria partners in the country.
Provincial coordination and roll out of BCC activities	TBD (Malaria bilateral)	800,000		Tete, Nampula, Zambezia, Cabo Delgado	Provincial level planning and implementation of BCC activities that build from the national level guidance. BCC approaches will employ multi-channel activities and evaluate their effectiveness in uptake of desired behaviors.
Faith based community BCC activities	PIRCOM	217,500		Nationwide	Support to the PIRCOM community level BCC networks to carry out malaria related IPC activities.
SUBTOTAL BCC		**1,217,500**			
MONITORING AND EVALUATION					

Proposed Activity	Mechanism	Budget Total $	Commodity $	Geographic Area	Description
Provincial level M&E support	MCSP (in Zambezia and Tete)	400,000		Tete, Nampula, Zambezia, Cabo Delgado	Working with provincial and district MoH counterparts, this support will build off existing information systems to improve the quality and completeness of facility data as well as its collection and use by district and provincial level authorities to improve programmatic decision-making.
	TBD (Malaria bilateral)	400,000			
DHIS-2 roll out	TBD (Malaria bilateral)	150,000		Maputo	Supporting the national effort to scale up and maintain the country's DHIS-2 management information system.
End-use Verification	TBD (Supply chain)	100,000		Nationwide	Continuing the development of EUV reports from supply chain data collected throughout the country.
CDC M&E Technical Assistance	CDC/IAA	20,000		Maputo	Three TDY visits by CDC M&E advisors to help the MoH better analyze and use programmatic data collected through its routine systems.
Durability monitoring	VectorWorks	200,000		Nampula	Funding for year three of ITN durability monitoring in Nampula Province. Includes final round of data collection, analysis and presentation of results.
SUBTOTAL M&E		**1,270,000**			
OPERATIONAL RESEARCH					
Impact of district level changes to vector control interventions	CISM	300,000		Zambezia	In light of the emergence of pyrethroid resistance throughout the country, this OR will provide crucial information on the effectiveness of vector control tools that still use these insecticides in comparison to different active ingredients.
SUBTOTAL OR		**300,000**			
IN-COUNTRY STAFFING AND ADMINISTRATION					
USAID	USAID	500,000		Nationwide	Support for two Foreign Service national malaria advisors, an administrative assistant and other Mission related costs.
CDC	CDC/IAA	550,000		Nationwide	Support for the CDC resident advisor and their administrative costs in addition to relocation funds due to staff turnover.
SUBTOTAL IN-COUNTRY STAFFING		**1,050,000**			

68

Proposed Activity	Mechanism	Budget		Geographic Area	Description
		Total $	Commodity $		
GRAND TOTAL		29,000,000	11,370,000